Glad to Meet You

THEODORE CLYMER
ROSELMINA INDRISANO
DALE D. JOHNSON
P. DAVID PEARSON
RICHARD L. VENEZKY

Consultants
CLAIRE HENRY
HUGHES MOIR
PHYLLIS WEAVER

Ginn and Company

0-663-38634-9

Acknowledgments: Grateful acknowledgment is made to the following publishers, authors, and agents for permission to use and adapt copyrighted material:

Crown Publishers, Inc., for "Henry Possum," text and selected illustrations, reprinted from *Henry Possum* by Harold Berson. Copyright © 1973 by Harold Berson. Used by permission of Crown Publishers, Inc.

Doubleday & Company, Inc., for "Mrs. Christie's Farmhouse," text and illustrations adapted from *Mrs. Christie's Farmhouse* by Caroline Browne, copyright © 1977 by Caroline Browne. Reprinted by permission of Doubleday & Company, Inc.

Elsevier-Dutton Publishing Co., Inc., for "The New Girl at School," adapted from *The New Girl at School* by Judy Delton. Text copyright © 1979 by Judy Delton. Reprinted by permission of the publisher, E. P. Dutton. Also for "Noises in the Woods," adapted from *Noises in the Woods* by Judi Friedman. Copyright © 1979 by Judi Friedman. Reprinted by permission of the publisher, E. P. Dutton. Also for "Socks for Supper," adapted from *Socks for Supper* by Jack Kent. Copyright © 1978 by Jack Kent. Reprinted by permission of the publisher, E. P. Dutton (A Parent's Magazine Press Book). Also for the poem "Waiting at the Window," with an illustration, from *Now We Are Six* by A. A. Milne. Copyright © 1927 by E. P. Dutton & Co., Inc., Renewal, 1955, by A. A. Milne. By permission of the publisher, E. P. Dutton.

Harper & Row, Publishers, Inc., for "A Nest of Wood Ducks," complete adapted text of *A Nest of Wood Ducks* by Evelyn Shaw. Text Copyright © 1976 by Evelyn Shaw. An *I Can Read* Book. By permission of Harper & Row, Publishers, Inc., and of World's Work Ltd, England.

Holt, Rinehart and Winston, Publishers, for the poem "January" from *Everett Anderson's Year* by Lucille Clifton. Illustrated by Ann Grifalconi. Copyright © 1974 by Lucille Clifton. Copyright © 1974 by Ann Grifalconi. Reprinted by permission of Holt, Rinehart and Winston, Publishers.

Little, Brown and Company for the poem "Adventures of Isabel," first ten lines, from *Many Long Years Ago* by Ogden Nash. Copyright 1936 by Ogden Nash. By permission of Little, Brown and Company.

Macmillan Publishing Company for "Emily's Bunch" by Laura Joffe Numeroff and Alice Numeroff Richter. Adapted with permission of Macmillan Publishing Company from *Emily's Bunch* by Laura Joffe Numeroff and Alice Numeroff Richter. Copyright © 1978 by Laura Joffe Numeroff and Alice Numeroff Richter.

Franklin Watts, Inc., for "Madge's Magic Show," adapted from *Madge's Magic Show* by Mike Thaler. Copyright © 1978 by Mike Thaler. Used by permission of Franklin Watts, Inc.

Associated Book Publishers Ltd, London, for the poem "Waiting at the Window," with an illustration, from *Now We Are Six* by A. A. Milne. Published by Methuen Children's Books Ltd. Reprinted by permission.

Ernest Benn Limited, England, for "Mrs. Christie's Farmhouse," adapted text, with selected illustrations, from *Mrs. Christie's Farmhouse* by Caroline Browne. Used by permission of the British publisher.

Curtis Brown Ltd., London, for the illustration accompanying "Waiting at the Window" from *Now We Are Six* by A. A. Milne. Line illustration by E. H. Shepard copyright under the Berne Convention. Reproduced by permission of Curtis Brown Ltd., London.

Curtis Brown, Ltd., New York, for "Helping" and "Farming," both adapted from *Partners* by Betty Baker. Reprinted by permission of Curtis Brown, Ltd. Text copyright © 1978 by Betty Baker. Also for "Emily's Bunch," adapted from *Emily's Bunch* by Laura Joffe Numeroff and Alice Numeroff Richter. Reprinted by permission of Curtis Brown Associates, Ltd. Copyright © 1978 by Laura Joffe Numeroff and Alice Numeroff Richter. Also for "Madge's Magic Show," adapted from *Madge's Magic Show* by Mike Thaler. Reprinted by permission of Curtis Brown, Ltd. Text copyright © 1978 by Michael C. Thaler. Also for the poem "January" from *Everett Anderson's Year* by Lucille Clifton. Reprinted by permission of Curtis Brown, Ltd. Text copyright © 1974 by Lucille Clifton.

Andre Deutsch Limited, London, for the first ten lines of the poem "Adventures of Isabel" from *I Wouldn't Have Missed It* by Ogden Nash. Published 1983 by Andre Deutsch. Reprinted by permission.

Dodd, Mead & Company, Inc., for the adaptation of "Morris Has a Cold" by Bernard Wiseman. Reprinted by permission of Dodd, Mead & Company, Inc. from *Morris Has a Cold* by Bernard Wiseman. Copyright © 1978 by Bernard Wiseman.

Follett Publishing Company for "Nobody Listens to Andrew," adapted from *Nobody Listens to Andrew* by Elizabeth Guilfoile, copyright © 1957 by Follett Publishing Company. Used by permission.

Berniece Freschet for "The Old Bullfrog," adapted from her book *The Old Bullfrog*. Text Copyright © 1968 Berniece Freschet. Published by Charles Scribner's Sons. Used by permission of the author.

Jean Marzollo for "A Visit to a Friend's House," adapted from her story "A Visit to a Blind Child's

(Continued on page 286)

Contents

3

Book-length Story

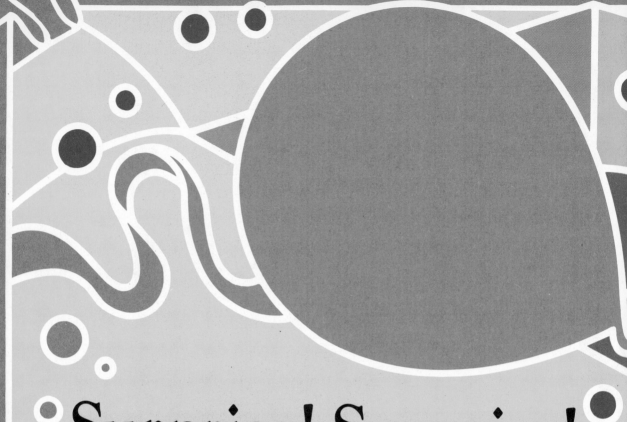

Surprise! Surprise!

People are fun to be with. They are interesting. People are surprising, too! Think of people you know. Have they ever surprised you?

You are about to meet some surprising people. Andrew will surprise you with what he has. Polly will surprise you with what she makes. Roberto surprises even himself. Emily surprises her brother Jeff. Maybe you'll be surprised, too!

9

Nobody Listens to Andrew

Elizabeth Guilfoile

Andrew saw something upstairs.
He ran down very fast. He said,
"Listen, Mom."

Mom said, "Wait, Andrew.
I must take Grandma to the bus.
She must get the bus before dark."

"Listen, Dad," Andrew said.
"I saw something upstairs."
Dad said, "Wait, Andrew.
I must cut the grass before dark."
"Nobody listens to me," thought Andrew.

Andrew said, "Listen, Ruthy.
I saw something upstairs. It was in my bed."
Ruthy said, "I can't stop now, Andrew.
I must find my bat and ball. I want
to play ball before dark."
"Nobody listens to me," thought Andrew.

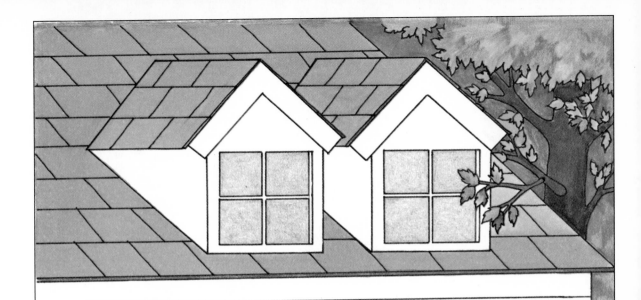

Andrew saw Mr. Pond walking his dog.

Andrew said, "Mr. Pond, I saw something upstairs.
It was in my bed. It was black."

Mr. Pond said, "I can't listen to you now, Andrew.
I must take my dog for a walk before dark."

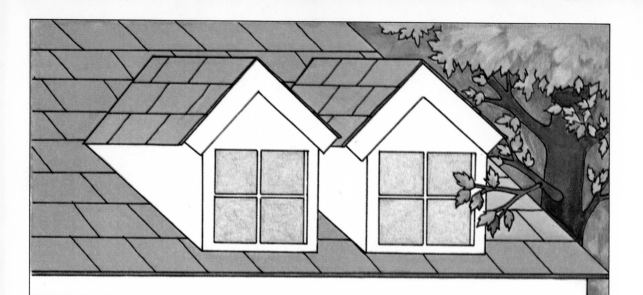

Andrew shouted, "Listen, Mom. Listen, Dad. Listen, Ruthy. Listen, Mr. Pond. Listen, Grandma. THERE IS A BEAR UPSTAIRS IN MY BED!"

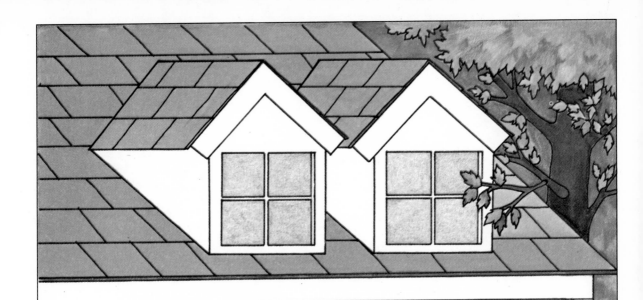

Mom stopped. She said, "Call the police."

Dad stopped. He said, "Call the fire house."

Ruthy stopped. She said, "Call the zoo."

Mr. Pond stopped. He called the police.
He called the fire house. He called the zoo.

Zoom! came the police.

Zoom! came the fire truck.

Zoom! came the woman
from the zoo.

15

They all ran upstairs. "Look!" said Mom. "It is black."

"Look!" said Dad. "It is in the bed."

"Look!" said Ruthy. "It's a bear! Andrew said it was a bear. But nobody listens to Andrew."

The police said, "It must have come from the woods. It climbed up the tree. It climbed in the window."

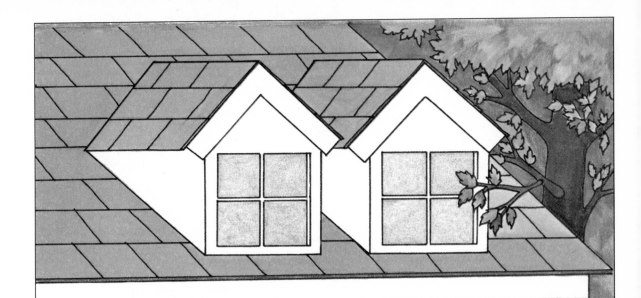

The woman from the zoo said,
"It is dry in the woods. The bears are looking
for water. I will take this bear to the zoo."

Everyone looked at Andrew. They all said,
"Next time we will listen to Andrew."

17

Rock Stew

Eve Rice

Polly knew just what to do this morning.
Today, she would make rock stew. She worked
all morning making rock stew. She made
other good things, too. It was a good morning
for making things.

When she was done, she put up a sign
that said, "LUNCH IS READY!" Next,
Polly beat on a pan with a spoon. She shouted,
"Lunch is ready! Lunch is ready!"

Willie could hear the noise all the way upstairs. He came out to look. "You are making so much noise," he said.

"That is because I'm open and ready for lunch," said Polly.

Willie looked at something strange. "What's that?"

"That is lunch," Polly answered.
"It's stew."

"It looks like mud to me," Willie said.

"It is rock stew," said Polly.

Willie looked again.

"It still looks like mud to me."

"Oh, but it isn't," Polly said.
"It is much better than mud. Would you
like some?"

"OK," Willie answered. "Some rock stew,
please."

Polly put some of the stew in a bowl.

"How much is that?" Willie asked.

"It's free to friends," answered Polly.

Willie put his spoon near his mouth and
made a strange noise.

"What are you doing?" Polly asked.

"Eating," said Willie. "Now I am
all done."

Polly looked in the bowl. "You're done?
It's still there."

"Well," said Willie, "that's the strange thing
about eating rock stew. There is just as much
in the bowl when you're done as when you started."

"Have you had enough?" Polly asked.

"Well," Willie said, "I could still
eat a sandwich."

"I could, too," said Polly.

22

Then they both went back into the house.

Serendipity

Eve Rice

Willie was thinking about getting something to eat. Polly walked by.

"Serendipity," Willie said.

"What's that?" asked Polly.

"A word," answered Willie. "I like the sound, but I don't know what it means."

"Let's find out," Polly said.

Polly and Willie went to the bookcase.

"The dictionary is gone," said Willie.

"Yes, but look," said Polly. "Here is my bell.
I was looking for it yesterday."

"It will not help us find what *serendipity*
means," said Willie. "Let's go."

They went to the desk. There were books
on the desk, and a flute. The dictionary
was not there.

"Oh," said Polly, "my train book!
I was looking for this. I thought I had lost it."

Just then Mrs. Brimble came home.

"Hello," called Mrs. Brimble.

Polly and Willie ran to see Mrs. Brimble.

"Do you know where the dictionary is, Mom?"
Willie asked.

"I think it's in the kitchen," answered
Mrs. Brimble.

Polly and Willie ran to the kitchen.
The dictionary was there.

Polly stopped by the sink. "Here is
my dark blue paint. I lost it this morning."

"Oh, your things get lost all the time,"
said Willie.

"Yes, but I find them again," Polly said.

"Let's find that word," said Willie.
They turned to the dictionary. When
they came to the word *serendipity*, Willie stopped.

"Let me see," said Polly.

She began to read: " 'Serendipity—
being able to find good things by accident.'
Well, I found my bell, my train book,
and my dark blue paint today—all by accident."

"Yes," Willie said, "and we found a
good word, too."

What Do You Do, Roberto?

Miriam Cohen

Roberto was upstairs working at
his fish tank. His brother and sisters
were getting ready to go to the Center.
They went every day they could. Today
Roberto was going, too. He couldn't wait.
This was the first time he was going to the Center.

At last his brother and sisters were ready.
Roberto was very happy.

"Hello, Roberto," said the woman
at the Center. "My name is Mrs. Sanchez.
You may call me Rosa. I know your sister Julia.
Julia said you would come today. Are you going
to play ball with Julia? She's good at playing ball.
Your sister Ana came today, didn't she?
You could go swimming with her. Ana is
very good at swimming. Do you know what
you're good at, Roberto?"

Roberto didn't know. He thought
and thought. He couldn't answer.

Roberto went to see what everyone was doing. He saw someone playing ball. "She's good at that," he thought. "What do I do well?" Then he saw people swimming. They were good, too. Every time he saw someone, he thought, "What can I do?" He still couldn't answer.

The next day nobody was playing ball. Nobody was swimming. Everyone was upstairs. Rosa was talking.

"The Center is going to have a party tomorrow," said Rosa. "Everyone can help get ready for the party."

Roberto thought a party would be fun. "What can I do to help?" he asked himself.

The next day everyone helped. Some people
made food. Others made a paper rainbow
and sun to put on the walls. Roberto's brother
and his friends helped to make some punch.
They made the punch in a great big pot.

Roberto thought, "How can I help?"

"Are you ready? The party's beginning!"
said Rosa. "Let's take the punch in now."

"Oh, no!" said Kate. "We made
the punch in this great big pot. We can't
pick it up. What can we do?"

"I can help," Roberto said.

"How can you help?" someone asked.

Roberto found a long straw. He put
some of the punch in the straw. He put a finger
over each end of the straw. Then he put
one end of the straw in the big pot. He put
the other end in a little bowl. The punch
ran out of the big pot into the bowl!
Now the party could begin.

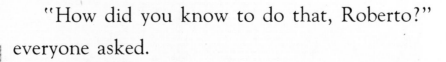

"How did you know to do that, Roberto?" everyone asked.

"At home I have some fish in a tank," said Roberto. "Every time the fish need new water, I use a hose. I put some of the water in the hose. I put a finger over each end of the hose. Then I put one end of the hose in the tank. I put the other end in a pan. I let the old water run into the pan. When I saw the pot, I thought that we could do the same thing with this punch."

Rosa looked at Roberto. "Now we know what you do well, Roberto," she said. "You're good at thinking."

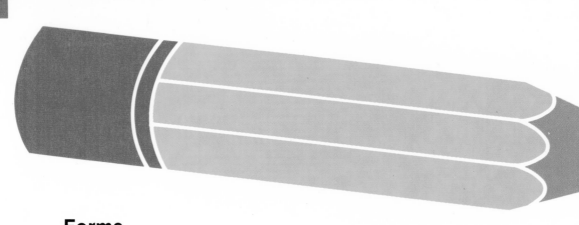

Forms

One day Roberto got a note from the Center. The next page shows the note from the Center. This kind of note is called a form.

What should you do with a form? First, read to find out what the form asks. Look for words that tell you how to write your answers. The Center's form tells you *Write yes or no.* This is how you should answer the questions. After you read the form, write an answer in each spot. Be neat and spell each word the right way. Then read your answers to be sure they are right.

Use what you have just learned to answer the Center's form. Write your answers on your paper. Write your name, address, phone number, and age. How should you answer the questions? What should you do after you write your answers?

About You

Name: _Roberto Gomez_   Phone: _555-1342_
Address: _24 Second Street_   Age: _8_

Write <u>yes</u> or <u>no</u>.

Do you have brothers and sisters? _Yes_

Things You Do

Write <u>yes</u> or <u>no</u>.

Do you know how to swim? _Yes_
Do you have a swim suit? _Yes_
Do you ride a bike? _Yes_
Do you like to play ball? _No_
Do you like to draw? _Yes_
Do you like to go to plays? _No_

Write each sentence using the correct word.

before   sister   brother   straw

Fire   Let's   every   ready

1. "_____ have a party," said Mrs. Sanchez.

2. "I have to be home _____ dark," said Tom.

3. "May I have a _____ for my drink?" asked Peg.

4. I read _____ book I can find.

Write the sentence that tells what will happen next.

5. Andrew is walking in the woods. He sees a small fire.

   a. Andrew plays ball.

   b. Andrew runs for help.

   c. Andrew goes swimming.

6. Polly wants to paint. Her paint is in the kitchen.

   a. Polly reads a book.

   b. Polly goes to sleep.

   c. Polly looks for her paint.

Write the word the sentence tells about.

stew   few   blew   drew   flew   chew

7. You do this when you eat.

8. A bird did this to get away.

9. The wind did this last night.

Read the sentences. Write *yes* if it could happen. Write *no* if it could not happen.

10. The girl is petting the kitten.

11. The fish is cutting the grass.

12. The house is hopping down the road.

A Visit to a Friend's House

Jean Marzollo

One day Rosa, who can see, stayed
with her friend Pat. Pat can't see.
She is blind. First, Pat and Rosa went
for a bike ride. Rosa rode her bike.
Pat rode on a tandem bike with her sister Gail.

When it was time to eat, they had chicken. Then they had apples. Pat couldn't tip her dishes over by accident. She had a special tray. This tray helped keep her dishes from tipping over.

Pat's bedroom was upstairs. She had
a bunk bed. Pat had the bottom bunk, so Rosa
got to sleep in the top bunk. The next morning
Pat showed Rosa her special trick for getting
dressed. She matched shape tags. There was a
round tag on her blue shirt. There was a
round tag on her dark blue slacks, too. The two
round shapes matched. That was how Pat knew
her colors would match.

Rosa asked, "How do you know which room you're in if you can't see?"

Pat answered, "I know my way around without seeing. I don't get lost. Sometimes if I get mixed up, I just stop and listen. Each room has a special sound.

"If I hear a clock, I know I'm in the living room. If I hear the water in the fish tank, I know I'm in the den. If I hear a bird singing, I know I'm in the kitchen. If I smell food being made, I know I'm in the kitchen, too. That's the room I like the best. It has the best noises and the best smells."

41

JANUARY

"Walk tall in the world,"
says Mama
to Everett Anderson.
"The year is new and
so are the days,
walk tall in the world,"
she says.

Lucille Clifton

Emily's Bunch

Laura Joffe Numeroff and Alice Numeroff Richter

Jeff wanted to go to Herbie's costume party.
He wanted to go dressed as Herbie.
Jeff thought it was a great idea.
Herbie thought it was awful.

Jeff's sister Emily wanted to go as a ghost.
Emily thought it was a great idea. Jeff thought
it was awful.

"I'll wear my costume tomorrow,"
thought Emily. "Jeff will see what a great costume
it is."

That's just what she did.

The next morning, Emily stood next to Jeff in her costume.

"I can't wait for him to see me," Emily thought.

Nothing happened.

Emily made strange noises and shouted, "Boo."

Jeff went on eating.

She shouted, "Boo," again.

Jeff got up and put his bowl into the sink.

"Aren't you afraid of ghosts?" Emily said.

"Who would be afraid of someone in a pillow case?" asked Jeff.

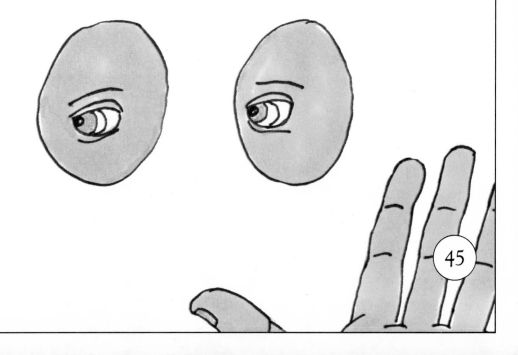

"I would," Emily said.

"Well," said Jeff, "I happen to know Peg is going as a ghost. So is Tim."

"Then I'll be a clown," said Emily.

"Well, I know Will is going as a clown," said Jeff.

"Then I'll be a rabbit," said Emily.

"Well, I know Lou is going as a rabbit," said Jeff. "Hank is, too."

"Then what can I be?" asked Emily.

"Nothing," said Jeff.

Emily thought for a while. "I know. I'll be a bunch of grapes. Nobody will be a bunch of grapes. It's a great idea."

"How are you going to be a bunch of grapes?" asked Jeff.

"You'll see," Emily said.

Every night Emily lay on her bed. She thought about how she was going to be a bunch of grapes. Nothing came to her.

"Oh, rats," she thought. "I'll bet Jeff has his Herbie costume by now."

On the night before the party, Jeff looked into Emily's room.

"I knew it," he said. "I just knew it. You're not a bunch of grapes. Wearing a purple bag does not make you a bunch of grapes."

"Oh, yes, it does," said Emily.

"Oh, no, it doesn't," said Jeff.

47

"Oh, yes, it does," said Emily's friends,
Julia, Kate, and Beth. They had on
costumes that matched Emily's.

"Oh, yes, it does," said Emily's other friends.
Ruthy and Joan jumped out. They had on
matching costumes, too.

"Wearing a purple bag DOES make you
a bunch of grapes. You just need other grapes
in your bunch!" said Emily.

From Head to Foot

Walker Stewart

Jeff and Emily made costumes for a party.
They were making them for fun. Other people
have costumes that they wear every day.
We just don't think of them as costumes.
People wear special hats and shoes for work.
People wear special hats and shoes for play.
In a way, the hats and shoes are
a kind of costume.

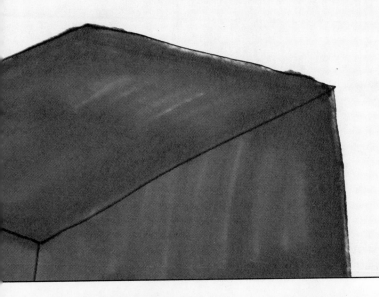

49

Hats and shoes can tell us a lot about people. They can tell us about the land where people live. They can tell us about the different kinds of work people do. They can tell us about how different people play. Let's take a look at some hats and shoes people wear every day.

Here is a woman who is working. Her hat tells you something about her work. She needs to keep her head covered. Her head is safe from danger because her hat is very hard. Does it surprise you that her hat is called a *hard hat*?

This man wears a hat to keep him safe from danger, too. He is called when there is a fire. When he jumps on his truck, he has his hat with him. He needs to cover his head. He will use a hose and water to put out the fire.

His shoes help him, too. They cover his feet and keep his feet dry.

Shoes can help people at work and at play.
Here is a different kind of shoe. This diver wears
shoes called *flippers*. Flippers help the diver swim
very fast. The diver may use flippers while
working. When the work is done, the diver
may want to swim for fun. Flippers are a big help.

People in other lands wear hats for work, too. Here is a man who is working. He is planting rice. Can you see how big and flat the straw hat is? The hat helps keep the sun out of the man's eyes. There is no danger of getting too much sun.

Here is a woman who wears a special hat to help her. She can put a jug of water on top of her hat. Then she can walk with the jug on her head. This leaves one of her hands free to do other work.

Shoes help people in other lands, too.
Holland is a very wet land because it is
near the sea. People there wear special shoes
made of wood when they work outside.
The shoes are hard and water can't get inside.
The shoes help keep people's feet dry.

It is hot all the time where some people live.
This man works outside in the sun. He wears
shoes with no toes to keep his feet cool.

Here are some different hats and shoes
people wear. Take a look and see how you think
people use them.

A Hole in the Dike

adapted from a story by Mary Mapes Dodge

Have you ever heard of Holland?
Holland is a land by the sea. In Holland
there are a lot of dikes. Dikes are like walls.
They keep the sea from coming onto the land.
Without dikes, Holland would be in danger. Water
would rush over the land and cover the ground.

The next tale didn't happen, but it could have.
It is about a boy from Holland.

57

One fine day, a boy ran along the top
of a dike. Night was coming. Soon he must
be home. He stopped to fling a stone into the sea.
The boy started to pick up another stone.
He stopped. What was that strange noise?
He stood still and listened. Plop, plop, plop.

He could hear the sound of water.

Looking down, the boy saw a stream of water.
Where could the water be coming from? There,
in the side of the dike, was a little hole.
Water was coming through the dike!

The boy knew the danger. More and more water
would stream through the hole. The hole would
get bigger. Soon the sea would rush through the hole
in the dike. Water would cover the land. Water would
cover his home. Something must be
done soon.

As fast as he could, the boy climbed
down the dike. He had an idea. He pushed his
hand into the hole. The stream of water stopped.

"Good," the boy thought. "The water can't
get in now. It will not cover my house."

Then the boy thought, "I need to go for help,
but I can't take my hand away. If I take my
hand away, the water will rush in." So he
stayed with his hand in the dike, calling for help.

Day turned to night. The sky was dark.
A cold wind blew. The boy shook with cold.

60

"Help! Over here!" the boy shouted.
No one heard him. No one came. The boy was
all by himself.

Soon the water turned his hand so cold that
he couldn't feel it. He became cold all over.
Soon the boy could feel nothing.

"How long can I last?" the boy asked himself.
"Why hasn't someone heard me calling?" He
thought of his home. He thought of his sister
and brother. He thought of his mother
looking for him.

He thought, too, of the dike. He knew
the water could cover the land. He was cold
and afraid, but he couldn't go home. He must
stay to save the land.

The sun came up. The sky turned yellow.
The boy could hear a sound. Someone was
walking on the dike!

"Here!" the boy shouted. "Come here!"
Someone looked down at him. It was
a woman.

"What are you doing? Are you lost?"
the woman asked.

"There's a hole in the dike. I'm keeping
the water back with my hand," said the boy.
"We must fix the dike. We must stop the water.
Get help as fast as you can."

Soon people came running down to the dike.
They began to fix the dike. When the work
was done, the people took the boy home.
Everyone was proud of him. He was
a very special boy. Last night, Holland had been
in great danger. Today, the danger was gone.
The water had not covered the land. The boy
had stayed all night to save Holland.

What's It All About?

You have read about the boy who saved Holland from danger. Now you will learn more about Holland.

TAKE A FIRST LOOK

A title tells what a story is about. It is written above the story. Look at the next page. What is the title of the story? What will the page tell you?

FIND THE KEY IDEAS

Look at the picture on the next page. It shows what a dike and a windmill look like. The title and the picture both tell you about the main idea of the page. What do you know about dikes and windmills?

READ CAREFULLY

Now read the next page. Read the sentences that tell about a dike. Then look at the picture. Read the sentences about windmills. How do dikes and windmills help Holland stay dry?

Dikes and Windmills Help Holland

Dikes and windmills help Holland stay dry. They keep water off the land. Find the dike and the windmill in the picture.

A dike is a low wall of dirt and rock. The wall keeps water from going onto the land.

A windmill has a pump inside. As the wind blows, the blades on the windmill turn. This makes the pump go. The pump draws water off the land. The water is pumped out to sea.

Windmills and dikes help keep the land in Holland dry. They make farming possible.

Write each sentence using the correct word.

1. I am wearing my new _____.

    match   shoes   danger

2. I _____ the birds singing.

    cover   nothing   heard

3. The dog will go away _____ you don't pat her.

    if   idea   costume

4. We like to swim in the cold _____.

    special   wear   stream

Write the best answer to each question.

5. Rosa is going to her friend's house to play. It is
cold outside. Rosa has nothing on her head.
What will Rosa do before she leaves?

    a. Rosa will play with her dog.

    b. Rosa will put on her hat.

    c. Rosa will eat an apple.

6. Emily wanted to ask Jeff about her costume. She heard him come into the house. What will Emily do next?

a. Emily will talk with Jeff.

b. Emily will go for a long walk.

c. Emily will feed her bird.

Write the answer to each riddle on your paper.

Decoding:
Vowel *oo*

brook   foot   hook   cook   hood   good

7. I get food ready for people to eat. I work in a kitchen. What am I? I am a _____.

8. I step from place to place. I help you run and walk. You cover me with a shoe. What am I? I am a _____.

9. I am water running through the woods. I am like a stream. What am I? I am a _____.

10. I am something you wear. You cover your head with me. I keep the cold and water out. What am I? I am a _____.

What's Going On?

Do you sometimes misunderstand what's going on? If you do, welcome to this unit! Just about everyone here has a misunderstanding. As you read, you will begin to understand what's going on.

The children in Room 12 use a code to tell about a surprise. They don't want to be understood—at least not right away!

Morris is misunderstood. Morris tells his friend Boris about a walking nose. Noses don't walk. A-CHOO! Boris helps Morris understand.

Winifred tries hard to be understood. If you understand what's going on, send her a sign!

WINIFRED

Anita Abramovitz

Winifred made things. She made
all kinds of things. She made old things,
new things, big things, and small things.

Winifred made a lot of things,
but she made them too fast. Some turned out
upside down. Others turned out inside out.

Winifred gave all the things away.
She gave them to everyone who lived on her street.

No one knew what to do with
Winifred's things. Everyone said,
"Thank you," but Winifred wasn't happy.
She knew they didn't mean it.

One day a woman who lived near Winifred
stopped her.

"Winifred," she said. "I know you want
to make things people can use.
Why not make signs?"

"Signs!" said Winifred. "What a good idea!"

Once Winifred had an idea, she never
wasted time. The next day she took a walk.
She looked and looked to see what there was in
the way of signs.

When she got back, she sat right down
and made her signs. But nobody could use the signs.
Nobody wanted them at all. So Winifred put
the signs around her house.

Soon people stopped in for eggs and apples. They asked if the house were for sale. They stopped in the morning. They stopped at night. Can you guess what that was like? Everyone got a bit mad and shouted at Winifred. So she took down all the signs.

That was not the end of it. Once Winifred started something, she couldn't stop. Every time she saw a sign, she had to make one like it.

Winifred took a walk to the zoo. When she got back, she sat right down to make signs.

Once again nobody wanted her signs. So Winifred put the signs up and down the street. She put them here and there, everywhere.

What a rainbow of colors! There were red and purple, green and blue signs everywhere. There were signs on the left. There were signs on the right.

The next morning, noise filled the street. Bells rang. Windows slammed. Winifred looked out. There was a fire truck in the street. There were police pulling down all of Winifred's signs.

73

Winifred wanted to run. Winifred wanted
to hide. Winifred wanted to fly away.
But Winifred was brave. She called from her window.

"Wait! Wait! Wait!"

Winifred rushed out.

"I'm sorry! I'm so sorry!" she said
to everyone. "I never thought this would happen!"

Soon everything was all right again.
The police left and took the signs with them.
The fire truck left, too. Now Winifred had a
new sign to make.

Winifred never wasted time. She got out
paper and paints. She made her best sign ever.
A friend helped Winifred put up her new sign.

WINIFRED'S SIGNS Made To Order

Soon, Winifred had more than enough to do. The first sign she made was for Beth's tree house. It said, "Keep Out." Then she made a sign in a rush for the house down the street. It said, "Bell not working. Please knock."

Now people say, "Thank you, thank you." Winifred isn't sorry. Winifred is happy because they mean it!

Morris
Has a Cold
Bernard Wiseman

Morris the Moose said, "I have a cold. My nose is walking."

Boris the Bear said, "You mean your nose is running."

"No," said Morris. "My nose is walking. I only have a little cold."

Boris said, "Let me feel your forehead."

Morris said, "Four heads! I don't have four heads!"

Boris said, "I know you don't have four heads. But this is called your forehead."

Morris said, "That is my ONE head."

"All right," Boris growled. "Let me feel your one head."

Boris put his hand on Morris's forehead.

Boris said, "Your one head feels hot. That means you are sick. You should lie down."

Morris lay down.

"Not HERE!" Boris shouted. "You are sick. You should lie down on a bed. Here is a bed. Come lie down. Put these covers on."

"No, no," said Boris. "Do not cover ALL of you.
Why did you cover your head?"

Morris said, "Because my head has the cold."

Boris said, "Your head should not
be covered." Boris took the covers from Morris's head.

".... A-CHOO!" Morris let out a big sneeze.

Boris covered Morris's head.

Boris asked, "How does your throat feel?"

Morris said, "Hairy."

"No, no," said Boris. "I don't mean outside.
How does your throat feel INSIDE?"

Morris opened his mouth to feel
the inside of his throat.

"No! No! No!" Boris shouted.
"Oh—just open your mouth. Let me look inside."

Boris said, "Your throat is red.
I know what is good for it. I will make you
some hot tea."

"Hot what?" asked Morris.

Boris said, "TEA. Don't you know
what tea is?"

"Yes," said Morris, "I know what it is.
T is like A, B, C, D . . ."

"No! No!" Boris cried. "Tea is . . .
Oh, wait—I will show you."

"This is tea," said Boris. Boris gave Morris
some tea. "Drink it. It will make your throat
feel better."

Morris said, "I am hungry."

"All right," said Boris. "I will make you something to eat. But, first, stick out your tongue."

Morris said, "I will not stick out my tongue. That is not nice."

Boris shouted, "Stick out your tongue!"

Morris stuck out his tongue.

"STOP!" Boris shouted. "That is not nice!"

Morris said, "I told you it was not nice."

Boris growled, "That's because you didn't do it the right way."

Boris looked at Morris's tongue. "Oh,"
Boris said. "Your stomach is upset."

Morris asked, "Did you see all the way
down to my stomach?"

"No," said Boris. "I did not see
all the way down to your stomach. I just saw
your tongue. Your tongue is white. When
your tongue is white, it means your stomach
is upset. I know what you should eat. I will
make you some soup."

"Some what?" asked Morris.

"Soup," said Boris. "Soup is—
Oh, wait—I will show you."

Boris said, "Here is some soup."
Boris fed Morris the soup. Boris ate
some soup, too.

Then Boris said, "It is getting dark.
Go to sleep. If your cold is better in the morning,
I will make you a big breakfast."

"A big what?" Morris asked.

Boris said, "Breakfast. Breakfast is—
Oh! Go to sleep!"

In the morning Morris said, "My nose
is not walking. My one head is not hot.
My cold is better. Make me a big breakfast."

"All right," said Boris. "But
you have to do something for me. . . ."

Morris asked, "What?"

"DON'T EVER GET SICK AGAIN!"

A Lost Donkey?

Turkish Folktale

"Hodja! Hodja!" cried the woman.
"Hodja, get up!"

There was a pause. The woman listened.
She could hear nothing. "Hodja!" the woman
cried again. "Get up. The donkey seller
has work for you. Hurry!"

Hodja stuck his head out the window.
"Good woman, what is all this about?"

"Hodja," said the woman, "you must hurry.
The donkey seller has work for you. He wants you
to take some donkeys to his brother at once.
Hurry now!"

"I will come right away," said Hodja.

Hodja climbed onto the back of his donkey,
Small One. Then he rushed to the house
of the donkey seller. There in the street
were nine donkeys, tied one behind the other.

"Ah, here you are!" cried the donkey seller.
"Hodja, I want you to take these donkeys
to my brother. He is waiting for them, so
don't stop on the way. You must be there
by dark."

"But what if the donkeys want to stop?"
asked Hodja.

"Let them stop for a drink, but don't let them
get away. There are nine donkeys here, and
your donkey makes ten. All must get to my brother
before night comes. Now off with you," said
the donkey seller.

Hodja tied the nine donkeys behind Small One.
Then he climbed on, calling to the donkeys.
"Come on, little donkeys. Let us be off!" he cried.

Clip, clop, clip, clop! Hodja and the donkeys
rode through the streets. Soon they were
on the open road. The sun was hot.
The air was dry.

Clip, clop, clip . . . Hodja could feel
the rope pulling. He turned around. The donkeys
were drinking from a small stream near the road.
"Very well, my friends. Drink away. Your throats
must be dry. I will stop, too." Hodja tied
Small One to a tree and lay down next to a rock.
Soon he was fast asleep.

A loud noise from Small One woke Hodja.
He jumped to his feet. "Oh, no!" he cried.
"My donkeys! Where are they?" Hodja ran
this way and that way. He called to the donkeys.
He looked behind every tree. He looked behind
every rock. At last he saw them. They were
a little way off, eating grass.

Hodja tied the donkeys again, one behind the
other. He climbed on the back of Small One.
"Now, are we all here?" Hodja asked, looking back.
"One, two, three, four, five, six, seven, eight,
NINE! NINE? The donkey seller said there were
TEN in all! Oh, no!" cried Hodja, "I have lost
a donkey!"

Hodja jumped off Small One and ran everywhere,
calling out. "Donkey! Donkey! Where are you?
Come, donkey! Here is some fine grass!" Hodja
found no donkey.

By now it was getting very dark. Soon
it would be night. Hodja left the donkeys
where they were. He rode off on Small One
to look once more. Hodja called and called.
He looked and looked. He could not find
the lost donkey.

It was now night. Hodja could not see the road. He could not find the lost donkey. He climbed down from Small One and sat down in the road. "I never should have stopped," thought Hodja.

Just then Hodja heard someone coming. He jumped to his feet and called, "Hello, who is there?"

"It is I," said the donkey seller. "Why have you stopped here?" he asked.

Hodja shook his head. "I'm sorry. I'm sorry," he said.

"Well, come on. Why are you sorry? What
is it?" asked the donkey seller.

Hodja's eyes looked down. "I have lost a donkey."

"You have WHAT?" cried the donkey seller.
"Let me see!" He walked down the row of donkeys,
counting. "One, two, three, four, five, six, seven,
eight, nine, TEN!" He looked at Hodja. "Hodja!
All of the donkeys are here!"

Hodja ran to the donkeys. He counted them, too. "One, two, three, four, five, six, seven, eight, nine, TEN!" Hugging the last donkey, he cried, "You came back! You came back!"

"Come, Hodja," said the donkey seller. "It is dark, and you must get these donkeys to my brother. This time I will ride with you. Let's go!"

Clip, clop, clip, clop. The donkeys rode off into the night.

Clip, clop, clip, clop. Through the noise of the donkey's feet came another sound. Hodja was singing. He was happy. What could be better? He was on his way, and he had TEN donkeys!

What's It All About?

This page will keep you from getting mixed up like Hodja.

TAKE A FIRST LOOK

Read the title on the next page. Then look at the picture and the example. These three things help you tell what kind of problems are on the page. What kind of problems do you think are on this page?

FIND THE KEY IDEAS

Look at the example. Which numbers do you add first? Which numbers do you add next?

READ CAREFULLY

When you do a math page like this one, write the problems just as they are. Write neatly. Use the example and the picture to help you work the problems. Then read your answers. Make sure they are right.

How Many in All?

Sara has 10 fish in one tank. She has 13 fish in another tank. How many fish does she have in all?

Example

Step 1. Add the ones.

$$\begin{array}{r} 10 \\ +13 \\ \hline 3 \end{array}$$

Step 2. Add the tens.

$$\begin{array}{r} 10 \\ +13 \\ \hline 23 \end{array}$$

ADD

1. $\begin{array}{r}15\\+12\\\hline\end{array}$	**2.** $\begin{array}{r}22\\+16\\\hline\end{array}$	**3.** $\begin{array}{r}25\\+32\\\hline\end{array}$	**4.** $\begin{array}{r}36\\+21\\\hline\end{array}$	**5.** $\begin{array}{r}33\\+20\\\hline\end{array}$
6. $\begin{array}{r}28\\+31\\\hline\end{array}$	**7.** $\begin{array}{r}47\\+22\\\hline\end{array}$	**8.** $\begin{array}{r}17\\+41\\\hline\end{array}$	**9.** $\begin{array}{r}13\\+46\\\hline\end{array}$	**10.** $\begin{array}{r}66\\+33\\\hline\end{array}$

Vocabulary:
Word
Identification

Write each sentence using the correct word.

hurry   should   tied   tongue   eight   stomach

1. My _____ is upset because I ate too much.

2. Your _____ is inside your mouth.

3. If you don't _____, you will be the last one there.

4. She _____ the donkey behind her house.

5. Seven comes before _____.

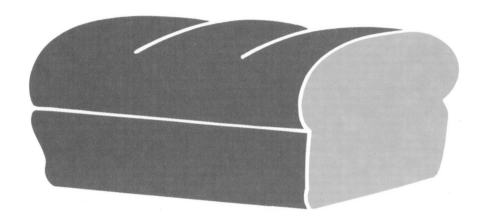

Vocabulary:
Vocabulary
Development
(multiple
meanings)

Write each sentence using the correct word. You should use each word two times.

sign   right   stick

6. My dog ran after the _____.

7. Stop your bike at the STOP _____.

8. The bread could _____ to the pan.

9. She never liked to use her _____ hand to paint.

10. I'm sorry that my answer was not _____.

11. Please _____ this paper.

Number your paper 12, 13, and 14. Write the sentences in the right order on your paper.

Comprehension: Sequence

Morris's throat is red.

Morris feels better.

Boris gives Morris some tea.

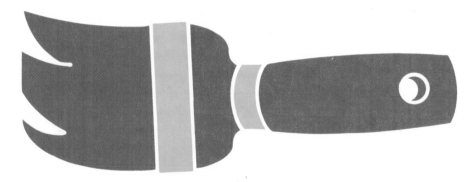

Write the first word. Then write the word with the same vowel sound as in the first word.

Decoding: Vowels *ie*, *i(gh)*, *au*, *au(gh)*, *o*

15.	lost	high	cause	boy
16.	tie	haul	bright	tongue
17.	off	tight	hope	sauce
18.	night	die	loss	paint

The New Girl at School

Judy Delton

My mother got a new job today.

I got a new school.

"It will be fun," said my mother.

"You will make lots of new friends."

When I walked into school,
everyone looked at me.

Everyone was friends with each other
but not with me.

I had on my new dress with the octopus.
(No one looked at the octopus.)

The teacher called me Martha.
(My name is Marcia.)

Everyone knew where the bathroom was.
(I had to ask.)

Everyone knew subtraction. (I didn't.)

"I don't like this school,"
I said to my mother that night.

"It will be better
tomorrow," she said.

The second day I sat by myself on the bus. (The seats were for two.)

Going to lunch, I was the only one standing by myself.

After lunch, we looked for oak leaves in the school yard. (I had to look by myself.)

"The second day was no better," I said to my mother that night. "I don't like being the new girl at school."

"Give it time," said my mother.

The next day I didn't want to go
to school. I cried and said my stomach
was upset. I cried and said I would run away.

My mother said, "Get on the bus."

At school we drew zoo animals.
The teacher showed everyone the best ones.
(He didn't show mine.)

We played Captain-May-I, and
I wasn't the captain. But when
we played baseball, I made it to second base.

That night my mother said,
"How was school?"

"Give it time," I said.

"Maybe I should talk to the teacher,"
she said.

"I'm too big for that now," I said.

99

The next day we made airplanes and
the teacher hung mine up. (He hung up only mine.)
  I was wearing my octopus dress, again.
Someone said, "Is that a snake?"
  I said, "No, it's an octopus."
  Emily asked me to her party.
(She could ask only eight.)

The next night, my mother said,
"You could stay with Grandma and go
to your old school."

"Why?" I said. "I like this one now.
And guess what? There was a new girl at school
today. She doesn't know subtraction."

Catch a Little Rhyme

Once upon a time
I caught a little rhyme

I set it on the floor
but it ran right out the door

I chased it on my bicycle
but it melted to an icicle

I scooped it up in my hat
but it turned into a cat

I caught it by the tail
but it stretched into a whale

I followed it in a boat
but it changed into a goat

When I fed it tin and paper
it became a tall skyscraper

Then it grew into a kite
and flew far out of sight . . .

Eve Merriam

Ways to Use Words

George W. Eichner

Do not use Pond Street.

Going on Land Road is the fastest way

to get home.

You speak, read a book, listen to the radio. These are ways to use words. You use words to tell how you feel or what you want. There are many other ways to use words.

Newspapers use words. You can read the newspaper to find out many things. You can find out if it will be hot or cold tomorrow. Do you know how a newspaper is made?

The radio is another way to find out things. The radio helps people at work and at play. Do you know how people use the radio at work?

This is the newspaper office in Eastfield.
The people working for this newspaper get the news.
They find out what is going on. Sometimes
they go to see the news while it's happening.
Then they write a news story for the paper.

Some of these people work in the office
in Eastfield. Others work in offices far away.
They write about the news in these places.

Some news is sad. You might read a story
about someone who lost a pet. Other news is happy.
You might read about someone who won a big prize.
People read about this prize in the newspaper.
One day you may write a news story for a newspaper.

Other people get the news ready for the press.
The press prints the newspapers. Then the newspapers
are ready to go to the trucks. The trucks rush
the newspapers all over Eastfield. The people
of Eastfield can read the newspapers. Some people
get their newspapers at a store. Other people
have their newspapers brought to their homes.
Do you get a newspaper at home or in school?

These people use a kind of radio at work.
Police and fire stations have two-way radios.
Do you know why they are called two-way radios?
This policewoman talks into her radio. Someone
at the police station can hear her. He talks back
into his radio. The sounds go two ways. That is why
they are called two-way radios.

This man drives a truck. Sometimes he uses
a two-way radio. How does the radio help him?

You may have a radio that is not two-way.
This kind of radio tells you many things.
You can find out the news. You can find out
if it will be hotter or colder tomorrow. A radio
is like a newspaper. It tells you what is happening.

Radios are for fun, too. You can listen to songs.
You can hear a great story. Do you like to listen
to the radio?

Newspapers and radios are just two ways
to use words. There are many other ways to use words.
Can you think of some other ways to use words?

A Note from
Room 12

Elaine Marcell

"Who can read a code?" Ms. Stone wanted to know. Nobody answered.

"Who knows what a code is?" she asked.

"I saw a code once. A code is another way of saying something, isn't it?" said Peg.

"Yes, it is," said Ms. Stone. "I have something for us to read. It's printed in code. It was brought to our room this morning from Room 12. Here it is."

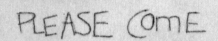

> PLEASE COME
>
> We have 1 new
> 4 21 3 11 12 9 14 7
> in our 18 15 15 13. It is
> small and yellow. It can
> swim, too. Could you 3 15 13 5
> to a little 16 1 18 20 25 to
> see it? Let us 11 14 15 23
> by tomorrow.
> Room 12

"Let's look at the code again and try to read it," said Ms. Stone.

"It looks funny," said Julia.

"It looks too hard to read," said Jeff.

"What could it say?" asked Tim.

112

"Can you guess why Room 12 sent us the note?" asked Ms. Stone.

"Well, it says 'Please Come,' " said Gail. "Maybe Room 12 is asking us to come to their room for something."

"That's a good beginning," said Ms. Stone.

"We said a code was another way to say something," said Tim. "Are the numbers showing us words in another way?"

"Yes. That's it!" shouted Jack. "Isn't it, Ms. Stone?"

"Yes," she said. "You're right."

"I think '18 15 15 13' means room," said Julia. "The note says they have something new. It must be in their room."

"You're all doing very well," said Ms. Stone. "The numbers do show words. But the numbers are not all the same. Why?"

"Room 12 wants to trick us," said Peg.

"No. I'll bet Room 12 wants us to work hard. If we can guess what the code says, we can find out the surprise," said Tom.

"Does each number stand for something?" asked Jack.

"Yes. It does," said Ms. Stone. "Let's look at the word Julia guessed."

"Can you tell what the numbers stand for?" asked Ms. Stone.

"Can they stand for letters?" asked Beth. "18 could stand for the letter *r*. Then 15 could be an *o*, and 13 could be an *m*."

"Good for you, Beth," said Ms. Stone.
"Every letter has a number to go with it."

"Oh, look," said Jo. "The first code word
only has one number. I think it is an *a*. A is 1."

"Why don't you all take some paper," said
Ms. Stone. "Write all the letters of the alphabet
on it. Then match the numbers with the letters
you know. Let's see if we can work out the code.
I'll work with you."

Before long everyone knew what they were
going to see. They had worked out the code.

This is what was on the note from Room 12.

PLEASE COME

We have 1 (a) new
d u c k l i n g
4 21 3 11 12 9 14 7
in our 18 15 15 13 (r o o m). It is
small and yellow. It can
swim, too. Could you 3 15 13 5 (c o m e)
to a little 16 1 18 20 25 (p a r t y) to
see it? Let us 11 14 15 23 (k n o w)
by tomorrow.

Room 12

Bob took a note back to Room 12.
This is what the note said.

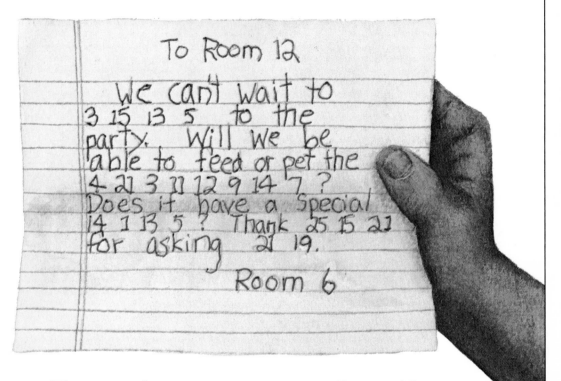

To Room 12

We can't wait to
3 15 13 5   to the
party. Will we be
able to feed or pet the
4 21 3 11 12 9 14 7 ?
Does it have a special
14 1 13 5 ? Thank 25 15 21
for asking 21 19.

Room 6

The next day everyone went to Room 12
for the party. They saw the yellow duckling.
They saw another code, too. This time everyone
could read the code. It said,

MY name is
8 5 18 2 9 5

117

Alphabetical Order

You have been reading about the pet duckling in Room 12. Do you have a pet at your school or at home? What kinds of animals make good pets? What if you wanted to make a list of them? You could put the words in a special order. Then each word would be easy to find. One kind of special order is alphabetical order.

Do you know the order of the letters of the alphabet? Then putting words in alphabetical order is easy.

Try the words *dog* and *frog*. Look at the first letter in each word. The first letters are *d* and *f*. Where do these letters come in the alphabet? The letter *d* comes before *f*. So *dog* comes before *frog* in alphabetical order. Which comes first in alphabetical order, *frog* or *cat*? Put these words in alphabetical order:

fox   bear   skunk   robin

Now look at *frog* and *fish*. Which word comes first in alphabetical order? The first letters are the same. This time you have to look at the second letters. Which comes first in the alphabet, *r* or *i*?

Put the names of these animals in alphabetical order. Write them on your paper.

toad   cow   rabbit   turtle   donkey   chicken

Which animal comes first? How did you know whether *cow* came before or after *chicken*?

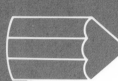
Write each sentence, using the correct word.

1. Our mother is a _____ at school.

　　radio　　number　　teacher

2. I will _____ to read the book by myself.

　　try　　or　　their

3. I would like to _____ a story.

　　forehead　　myself　　write

4. _____ people walk their dogs.

　　Try　　Code　　Many

Write the first sentence. Then write the sentence in which the word *second* or *letter* has a different meaning.

5. She was the **second** one here.

　　a.　The **second** story was the best.

　　b.　A **second** is not a long time.

6. We will write a **letter** to our teacher.

　　a.　My name begins with the **letter** M.

　　b.　I have a **letter** here from my mother.

Write the sentences in the right order.

Comprehension: Sequence

7. Marcia hit the ball hard.

We started to play baseball.

Marcia ran to second base.

8. Then Jeff went back to school.

Jeff saw all the animals at the zoo.

Jeff walked to the zoo from school.

Write each sentence, using the correct word.

Decoding: Inflections -er, -est

9. My donkey is _____ than your donkey.

big   bigger   biggest

10. The soup is too _____ to eat.

cold   colder   coldest

11. An airplane goes _____ than a van.

fast   faster   fastest

12. That is the _____ sign on this road.

big   bigger   biggest

Imagine That!

Abracadabra! The magic carpet of your mind wants to take you on a trip through this unit. Let your imagination go . . . to laughter, to fun, to mystery.

Be sure to stop at Madge's. She has lots of things up her sleeve and in her hat. Then on to fun and mystery. Join some friendly animals on their way to Bremen. They band together and play a special tune! On the way, you can make music, too. Tap your feet. Whistle a song. Clap your hands.

Are you ready? Get set for a race . . . a kind of race only you can imagine!

Waiting at the Window

These are my two drops of rain
Waiting on the window-pane.

I am waiting here to see
Which the winning one will be.

Both of them have different names.
One is John and one is James.

All the best and all the worst
Comes from which of them is first.

James has just begun to ooze.
He's the one I want to lose.

John is waiting to begin.
He's the one I want to win.

James is going slowly on.
Something sort of sticks to John.

John is moving off at last.
James is going pretty fast.

John is rushing down the pane.
James is going slow again.

James has met a sort of smear.
John is getting very near.

Is he going fast enough?
(James has found a piece of fluff.)

John has hurried quickly by.
(James was talking to a fly.)

John is there, and John has won!
Look! I told you! Here's the sun!

A. A. Milne

Madge's Magic Show

Mike Thaler

Madge was very special. She was
a great magician. She had a hat, a cape,
and a wand. She even had a stage.

One day she wanted to give a magic show.
Everyone came from miles around.
Jimmy Smith didn't. He just looked
over the fence.

Madge waved her wand.

"Abracadabra. Frogs and Toads.
Girls and Boys, hello!
Get set to see some magic.
Here's Madge's Magic Show!"

Everyone clapped. Jimmy Smith didn't.
He looked away.

"For my first trick," Madge said,
"I will turn water blue." She did,
and everyone cheered.

"That's not so hard," said Jimmy Smith.

Madge looked over the fence at Jimmy.
Then she turned her back.

"I will now pull six hats
from this empty box," and she did.

Everyone clapped.

"Hats are nothing," said Jimmy Smith.

Madge stuck out her chin.
She pushed back her cape, and took off
her hat. She turned to face Jimmy.
"If you will stop talking," she said,
"I will do my best trick. It is a trick
never seen before on our street. I will pull
a rabbit out of this empty hat!"

"You can't pull a rabbit out
of an empty hat," said Jimmy Smith.

Madge said her magic words.
She reached into her hat, and pulled out . . .
a chicken!

"That's great!" said May.

"A chicken is not a rabbit,"
said Jimmy Smith.

"Give me a little time," said Madge.

She waved her wand.

She reached back into her hat.

She said the magic words, and pulled out . . . a fox!

"Well!" said Jimmy Smith.

"That's not a rabbit."

129

Madge waved her hand. She reached
into her hat, and pulled out . . . a goat!
Everyone laughed.
"I knew she couldn't do it!"
said Jimmy Smith. "She's not a magician."
"One more time," Madge said.
She paused. Then she reached again
into her hat. She said the magic words.
She pulled out . . . a cow!
"Wow! A real cow," said everyone.
"I just knew she couldn't do it,"
said Jimmy Smith.

Madge put on her hat. "I guess
the show is over," she said.

Just then the hat began to rock.
A little pink nose stuck out from
under the hat.

"A rabbit!" said Madge.
"What took you so long?"

The little rabbit hopped to the ground.
Everyone clapped and cheered.

"Gee," said Jimmy Smith.
"A real rabbit. How did you do it?"

"It was nothing," said Madge,
tapping her hat. "All great magicians
know how."

Fun with Magic

Jesse Lynch

Madge had fun being a magician. You
can be a magician, too. Here's a magic trick
you can surprise your friends with.

What You Need

You will need three small cups you can't
see through. Paper cups work well. Then
you will need two small balls of cotton.

You must do two things before you show your friends this trick.
1 First, hide one piece of cotton in one of the cups, as you see here.
2 Then, place the cups inside each other with the cotton in the middle cup. Now you can begin the trick.

What You Do

Show your friends the other piece of cotton. Then flip the cups over fast, one by one. You have to do this fast so the cotton doesn't drop out of the cup.

What You Say

I have here some cotton and three cups.

Put the cups next to each other. The cup with the cotton in it should go in the middle. Put the other piece of cotton on top of the middle cup.

Now put the other two cups on top of the middle cup. When you take away the cups, your friends will see the cotton. (They'll think it's the cotton you put on *top* of the cup. Only you know it's the first piece of cotton you put *inside* the middle cup.)

What I'm going to do is put this cotton on top of this cup.

Next I will put the other two cups on top of the middle cup.

Now I will make the cotton go through the cup!

Abracadabra! It's magic!

THE MYSTERIES OF SCIENCE

Jane Bade

Magic is like a mystery. Magic tricks our eyes. Magic can make things seem to go away. Magic can show us something we didn't see before.

Many things that happen every day look like magic. They are really mysteries of science. Here are some things for you to try.

Rainbows

A rainbow is a mystery of science.

Think about it. Where does a rainbow come from? Where does it go? When the sun shines through the rain, we see beautiful colors in the sky. Every rainbow has the same colors—purple, blue, green, yellow, orange, red. Where do the colors come from? Where do they go?

You can make a rainbow. You can make rainbow colors in your room. Put a pan of water in the sunlight. Shake the pan. Can you see the colors jump across the walls of the room?

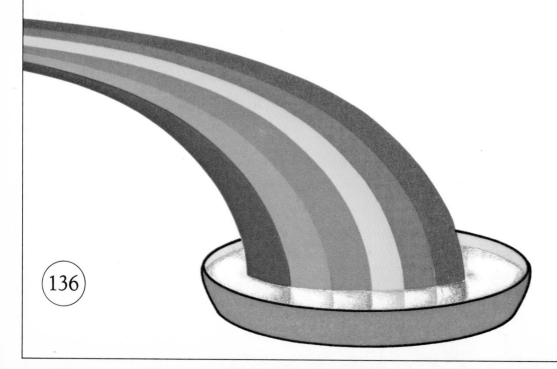

Size

Every day we see things that are not
what they seem to be. Sometimes size
can fool us.

Look at an airplane in the sky.
The airplane looks smaller than a bird.
But you know it's really very big.
It's big enough for many people
to be inside.

137

Look at the frogs, caps, and hat.

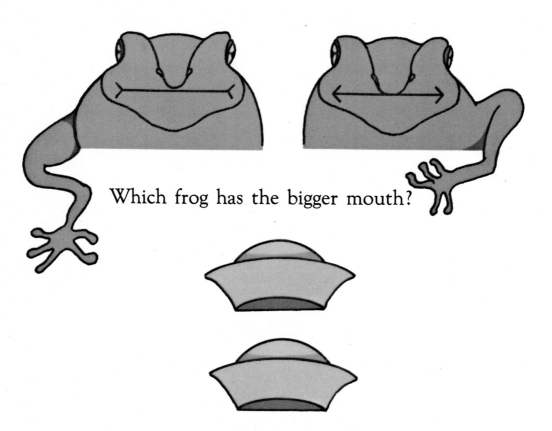

Which frog has the bigger mouth?

Which of these two caps is bigger?

Is the hat taller than it is wide?

Do you know the answers to these mysteries? Here's an idea to help you. Use a piece of paper to find out how long the lines are.

The mouths of the frogs are the same size. The two caps are the same size. The hat is as wide as it is tall.

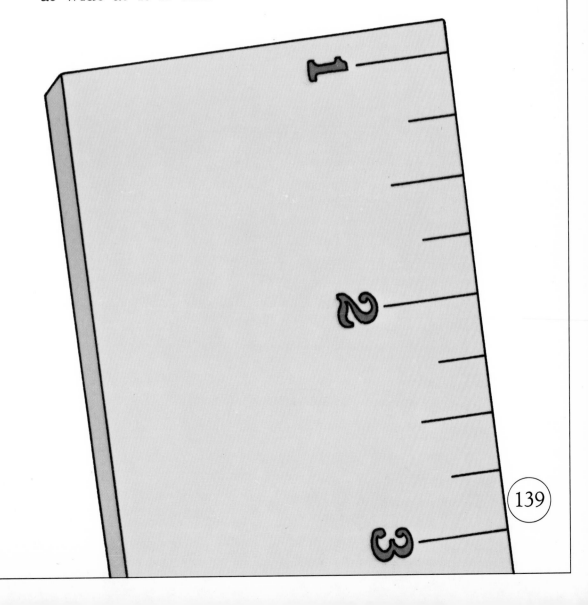

Put a coin in a glass of water. Look at the coin from the top. What size is it? Look at the coin from the side. Does it look the same size now? Why not?

Here's a trick that looks like magic. Look through the glass like this.

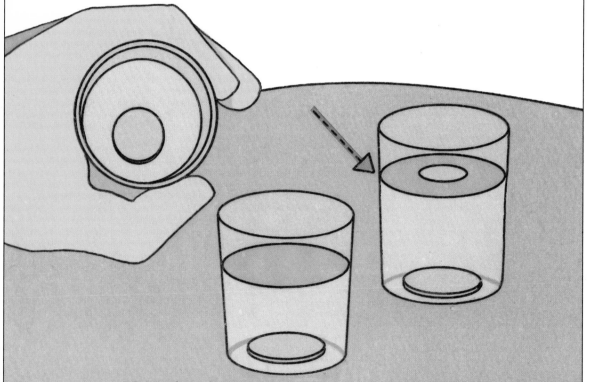

You should see a big coin on the bottom of the glass. Another coin seems to be on top of the water.

Hot and Cold

Put three bowls in a row. Put hot water
in the first bowl. Put warm water in the middle bowl.
Put very cold water in the last bowl.

Now place one hand in the hot water. Place
the other in the cold water. Leave them both there
for a while. Then put both hands in the bowl
of warm water. What happens?

One hand should feel that the water is cold.
The other hand should feel that the water is hot.
Why do you think that is happening?

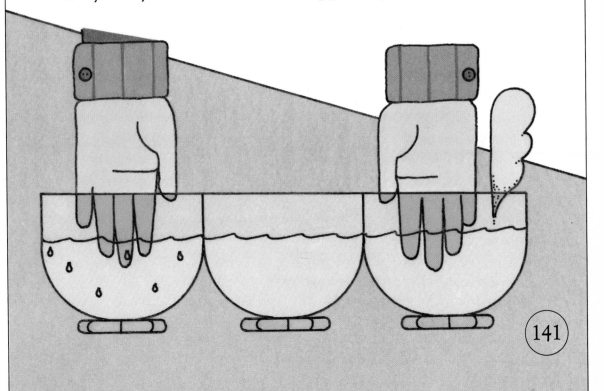

Mystery Ink

You can use science to write a mystery note.
Only the friend you give it to will know how
to read it.

You can make ink that no one can see.
Use milk, a stick, and some paper. Dip the stick
into the milk. Write your letter on the paper.
When it is dry, no one can see the words.
The words will show up only when the paper is hot.
Put the paper near a light to make it hot. Now
you can see the letters.

These are only some of the mysteries of science.
There are so many more! You can see a rainbow
in a spot of oil. A toy near you will seem
bigger than a toy far away. Look at your legs
the next time you're standing in water!

The mysteries of science may seem like magic,
but they are not magic. We know now that
some things are not what they seem to be!

143

Socks for Supper

Jack Kent

Far away and long ago there
lived a husband and wife. All they had
was a small house and a little beet garden.
One day, the husband said to the wife, "I'm sick
of eating nothing but beets. I won't eat
another beet."

Nearby lived Mr. and Mrs. Whipple.
Mr. and Mrs. Whipple had a cow. The husband
and the wife used to look at the cow. They
dreamed of milk and cheese. "Maybe
Mr. and Mrs. Whipple will sell us some milk
and cheese," said the husband.

"No, they won't. We don't have any
money," the wife said to him. "Maybe
we could trade them something for some milk."

"Maybe we could," the husband said. They
looked all over the house for something to trade.
They looked and looked. The only thing they
could find was a pair of socks.

The husband took the socks and went to see
Mr. and Mrs. Whipple. In a little while
the husband came home again. He was very happy.
He had a whole pail of milk and a small cheese.
"Oh! This is so good!" said the wife.

Before long, the husband and the wife
began to wish they had more milk and cheese.
But they didn't have any more socks to trade.
"I will knit some socks!" said the wife.
But she didn't have any yarn. So she
took some yarn from the husband's sweater.
She knit a pair of socks with the yarn.

147

The husband went again to trade the socks
for milk and cheese. Again they feasted as
they had before.

When the food was gone, the wife
knit another pair of socks. She used some more
yarn from the husband's sweater. Again the
husband went to trade the socks for milk and cheese.

When the food was gone, the wife
started to knit again. Now there was
only enough yarn left from the sweater
to make one sock.

"What good is one sock?" the wife asked.
"They won't trade any milk or cheese for that."

"We'll see," said the husband. And he took
the sock to the people with the cow.

"I only have one sock this time," he said.
"Would you trade half a pail of milk and
half a cheese for it?"

"Fine," said Mr. Whipple.

"You see," said Mrs. Whipple, "One sock
is just what I need."

She had started to knit Mr. Whipple a sweater.
She had used the yarn from the socks. She needed
just one more sock. Then the sweater would be done.

But the sweater really didn't fit Mr. Whipple.
So Mrs. Whipple gave the sweater to the husband.
She had seen that the husband didn't have one.
And it was just the right size for him!

151

Introductions

In the last story, the husband went to see Mr. and Mrs. Whipple. He wanted to trade with them for some milk and cheese. First, he had to tell them who he was. He had to introduce himself.

Do you know how to introduce yourself?

Won't you say hello to Carmela? She is about to introduce herself to you!

Hello! My name is Carmela.

I live on Spring Street.

What is your name?

What would you say to Carmela?
When you introduce yourself, it is important
to tell your name. You can tell something else
about yourself, too. What else did Carmela
tell you about herself? What else do you
like to know about new friends?

Make believe you are meeting Carmela
for the first time. Introduce yourself to her.
Did you tell her something new about yourself?
It is great to make new friends!

153

Vocabulary:
Word
Identification

Write the words in the order that makes a sentence.

1. waved   The   magician   his   wand   .

2. I   mysteries   like   read   to   .

3. wear   size   What   you   sock   do   ?

4. science   have   Do   books   you   any   ?

Vocabulary:
Vocabulary
Development
(synonyms
and antonyms)

Write *same* if the words have almost the same meaning. Write *opposite* if the words have opposite meanings.

5. big—little

6. before—after

7. hurry—rush

8. hard—soft

9. center—middle

10. wish—want

Write the sentences. Write *real* or *make-believe* next to each sentence.

Comprehension:
Reality and
Fantasy

11. The woman knit a pair of socks.

12. The cow knit a sweater.

13. Tom reads his science book every day.

14. Cats write mystery books.

Write each sentence using the correct word.

Decoding:
Consonants *g*,
scr, spr, str, wh;
Vowels *oi, oy*

wheels   happy   stroll   boil   age   read

15. To feel joy is to be _____.

16. Gail wanted to _____ water to make some tea.

17. Roy heard the screech of the truck's _____.

18. Peg spread open the pages of the book and started to _____.

Let's Make Music

Marion Miller

Did you ever blow air over the top
of a bottle? How did it sound? Was it
a big bottle or a small bottle? Do you think
all bottles would sound the same? Do you think
the size of the bottle would change the sound?

When someone plays a flute, the same thing
happens. The player blows air over a hole
in the flute. This makes a musical tone or sound.

The player can change this tone by opening
more holes in the flute.

A recorder is a flute, but it is played up and down.
All flutes used to be played like a recorder. Now,
most flutes are played the way the boy is playing his.

Many people today like to play music
on a recorder.

Try making music with a piece of string.
Tie one end of a piece of string to something
that won't move. Hold the end of the string
in one hand. Pull it tight. Now pluck the string
with your other hand. The string should spring back
into place. You really can make a musical tone
with a piece of string!

Now pull the string really tight. Pluck
the string again. How does the tone change?

This player is pulling the strings of a banjo
tight. The strings will make musical tones
when she strums the banjo.

With her hand, the banjo player makes
some of the strings shorter. Do you think
this would change the musical tones?

Do you like to clap your hands? Do you like
to tap your feet? Doing these things is like playing
a drum. When you tap your feet, you use the floor
as a drum.

You can make a drum. You can use lots of things
to make one. Find a box or a can. Tap on it
with your hands or a stick.

What other ways can you make a musical tone?
Scrape the top of the drum. Tap with a hard beat.
Tap with a soft beat. Tap fast. Tap slowly. Put
something inside the box or can. Listen to
the tone change. You are playing a drum!

159

There is one musical instrument everyone has.
Can you guess what it is?

That's right! Your voice is a musical instrument.
You can take your voice with you everywhere you go.
When you sing, you use your voice to make musical
tones. You can make any tone your voice can make.

Some people think the voice is the most beautiful
instrument of all!

Music is all around us. Where do you hear music?
What kind of music do you like most?
What musical sounds do you like to hear?

Jacob and Wilhelm Grimm as retold by Harry Allard

On the Way to Bremen

There once was an old donkey named Grace.
Now Grace was getting on in years. Her ears were
gray, and she had to walk with a cane.

One day as Grace was going to the mill,
her cane broke. "Enough is enough," Grace said.
"I can't work at this mill another day!"
That very night Grace left for the City of Bremen.

"They like music in Bremen," Grace said.
"I am a banjo player. I will play my banjo there."

She had not gone very far when she met
a dog named Captain. Captain was getting on
in years, too. He was in a wheelchair.
"I can't hunt any more," said Captain, "so
I just play my drum."

"Let me push you to Bremen," Grace said.
"I will play the banjo," she said, "and
you can beat the drum."

163

Soon Grace and Captain met a cat named Jane.
She was humming a cat song. Jane, too,
was getting on in years. She had on thick glasses.
Jane said, "I just can't see the mice any more."

"Forget the mice, Jane," said Grace, "and
come to Bremen with us."

"But what can I do in Bremen?" asked Jane.

"You can sing," said Captain.

Jane went with Grace and Captain.

On the road to Bremen, the three animals met
a rooster on a bike. The rooster's name was
Mr. Sanderson. "I have lived at my old farm
most of my life. I need a change," Mr. Sanderson said.
"I'm on my way to find a new farm."

"Forget a new farm," said Jane.
"Come with us to Bremen. You can tap-dance
with our Bremen City Band. We'll all ride with you
on your bike."

The City of Bremen was far away.
The four animals rode a long time. Night came.
With all the animals on his bike, Mr. Sanderson's
legs gave out.

They came to a house. Now in this house,
there were three robbers. They were counting
the loot they had brought back to the house
that day. Looking in the window, Jane said,
"Am I really seeing robbers?"

"Yes, you are," said Captain.

"You really are," said Grace.

"No question about it," said Mr. Sanderson.

"I have a good idea," said Jane. "Grace
will play her banjo. Captain will beat his drum.
Mr. Sanderson will tap-dance, and I will sing.
With all the noise, the robbers will run for
their lives."

So Grace played her banjo. Captain beat
his drum. Mr. Sanderson did a tap dance, and
Jane sang.

The robbers in the house shouted in fright.
They had been found! The robbers ran away and never
came back. So the donkey, the dog, the cat, and
the rooster stayed. They never did make it to Bremen.
They were really too happy to leave.

Dictionary

You have just read about some musical instruments. You learned about a *banjo,* a *drum,* and a *recorder.* What if you did not know what a *banjo* was?

You can find the meaning of a word in a dictionary. A dictionary is a book that tells about words. It is a big, long list of words in alphabetical order. The words beginning with *a* are in the front. The words beginning with *z* are at the end.

To help you find words quickly, two guide words are on the top of every page. One guide word tells what word begins the page. The other tells what word ends the page. All the words on the page come between those two words in alphabetical order.

The next page shows part of a dictionary. What are the guide words? Find the word *banjo.* It is written in dark letters. Then comes the respelling of the word—(ban′jō). This tells how to say the word. Next comes the meaning. What is the meaning of *banjo*?

air·plane (er′plān) a machine that flies through the air.

al·pha·bet (al′fə bet) the letters used to write words.

an·i·mal (an′ə məl) a living thing that can move and feel.
a·sleep (ə slēp′) not awake.

ban·jo (ban′jō) a musical instrument with strings.

base·ball (bās′bôl′) a game played with a bat and a ball.

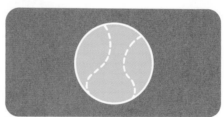

be·fore (bi fôr′) in front of.
Bre·men (brem′ən) a city in Germany.

Answer these questions on your paper. Use the dictionary words above.

1. What does the word *animal* mean?

2. What word comes after the word *before*?

3. Why does the word *alphabet* come after the word *airplane*?

4. Why isn't the word *bun* on this page?

Helping Betty Baker

Long ago when the world was new,
Badger was putting stars in the sky.
The bag of stars was big and lumpy.
The ladder was long, but Badger was
very strong. He was neat. He put out

the stars in the right order.

Coyote was singing to the new moon. Badger
went by, pulling the bag and the long ladder.
Coyote said, "Is there something to eat in that bag?"

"No!" said Badger. "I am not going to eat now.
There will be a dance when I am finished.
I will eat then."

"I will go to the dance with you," said Coyote.

Badger said, "Only those who help will go
to the dance."

Coyote did not want to help, but he wanted
to go to the dance. "We are partners," he said
to Badger. "You need a partner to move
the ladder and hold it for you."

"I can do that myself," said Badger.

"Yes," said Coyote, "but if I do it, you can
just think about the stars and how to put them."

"All right," said Badger. "You can help me."

Badger took some stars and went up the ladder.
He put out the stars, one by one. Then he came down.

"It's very pretty," said Coyote, "but make
it bigger."

He moved the ladder. Up went Badger.
Up went the stars, one by one.

"That is bigger," said Coyote, "but use more stars."

Coyote moved the ladder, and Badger went up
again. He was there a long time. He used a lot of
stars, and he put them out, one by one.

"Can't you do it faster?" said Coyote.

"No," said Badger. "The sky must be neat.
The stars must go up in the right order."

Again and again, Coyote moved the ladder.
Again and again, Badger went up and put the
stars out, one by one.

Everyone was getting ready to go to the dance
but Badger. He was still putting up stars.
Coyote could smell the food cooking.

"Hurry," said Coyote. "We will miss the dance."

But Badger put the stars out, one by one.
Coyote couldn't wait any longer. He took the bag.
He told Badger, "A partner should make things easy
for you. I will show you a better way." And
he threw the stars all over the sky.

"The sky is a mess!" said Badger.

"But we are finished," said Coyote.
"Now we can go to the dance." And they did.

Coyote told everyone, "Badger and I are partners. We put up the stars. Badger put up the pretty ones, but I put up the most." Then he ate and sang and danced and ate.

But Badger dug a hole in the ground so he would not see the messy sky.

Farming

Betty Baker

Coyote liked to eat melons, all kinds of melons. But he did not have any.

Badger had a farm. Coyote went to Badger and said, "We are partners. We should farm together."

"All right," said Badger. "Help me dig."

"No," said Coyote. "I am not good at digging. You are. You dig. I will do the planting."

"No," said Badger. "If you plant, you will make a mess. I will dig and plant. You pull the weeds."

Coyote said, "A partner should make things easy for you. You live in a hole, so you take everything that grows under the ground. I will just keep what grows on top."

"All right," said Badger, and he started to dig. Coyote put his tail up and went away laughing.

When it was time to pull weeds, Coyote was making a new song. So Badger pulled the weeds.

When it was time to pull them again, Coyote was singing his new song to the full moon. Again Badger pulled the weeds. Then Coyote went away to hunt rabbits. Badger pulled all the weeds.

When it was time to eat melons, Coyote
came back. The plants were big and green.
But they had no melons.

"You took my melons!" said Coyote.
"You only get what grows under the ground.
Give me my melons."

Badger said, "You did not tell me you
wanted melons. I planted what I always plant."

"What is that?" said Coyote.

"Potatoes," said Badger. Then he
dug them up and ate them all winter.

Winter passed. Spring came.

Coyote said, "It is not right
for one partner to get everything."

Badger said, "It is not right
for one partner to do everything."

"You are right," said Coyote. "You dig
and plant. I will pull the weeds. This time,
I will take what grows under the ground."

"All right," said Badger, and he
started to dig. Coyote put his tail up and
went away laughing. He did not come back
until it was time to eat potatoes.

Ha Ha Ha

The plants were big and green. Coyote dug
and dug. But the plants had no potatoes.

"Where are my potatoes?" said Coyote.

Badger said, "You did not tell me you wanted
potatoes. Last time you wanted melons, so
that is what I planted." And he dried
the melons and ate them all winter.

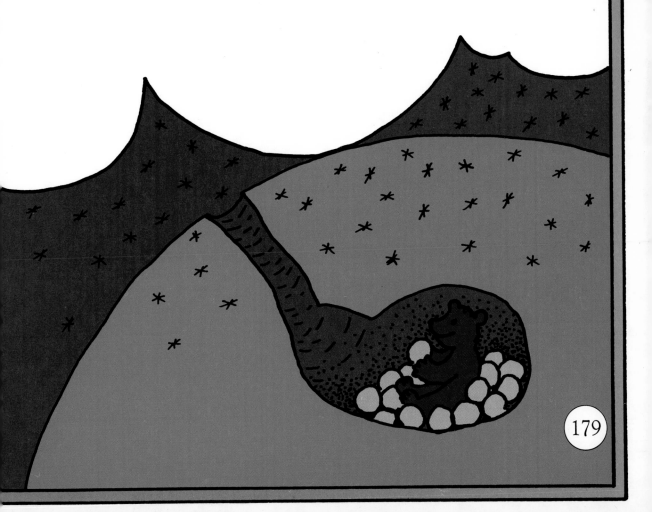

179

Vocabulary: Word Identification

Write each sentence, using the correct word.

1. The player strums the strings of a _____.

rooster   laugh   banjo

2. We _____ the rooster Fred.

year   named   pair

3. It's a mystery to me how potatoes and _____ grow.

winter   melons   ladder

4. The stars moved across the cold _____ sky.

potatoes   winter   mysteries

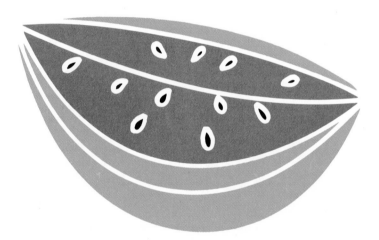

Vocabulary: Vocabulary Development (synonyms and antonyms)

Write *same* if the words have almost the same meaning. Write *opposite* if the words have opposite meanings.

5. questioned—asked

6. cried—laughed

7. look for—hunt

8. pair—two

9. over—under

10. won't—will

Read the story. Write the two sentences that tell what could not happen.

11. Gail liked to play music. Today, Gail was strumming on her banjo. A badger came up and started to play his flute. Gail started to sing while she played the banjo. The badger cried,"I don't know the words!"

Write the answers to the questions.

One day, a stray coyote came to Badger's house. Badger had a huge garden. "May I help you in the garden?" asked Coyote. "You can water the garden. The soil needs to be moist all the time," said Badger. They worked all spring. One day, Coyote pointed to the garden. "Look, Badger," cried Coyote. "We have a sprout pushing through the soil!"

12. Which word tells us Coyote didn't have a home?

13. What needed to be moist all the time?

14. What did Coyote see coming up in the garden?

Let's Go Places

Now let's go outdoors—to a farm or the woods.

Many animals live in the woods. In these stories you will meet some of these animals. You will meet bears, ducks, and bullfrogs, to name just a few.

Other animals live on farms. You will read about them and a very special goose, too.

People also live outdoors. Sometimes they get along well with animals. Sometimes they don't. What happens when Herman meets a bear in the woods? To find out, read on.

Not **THIS** Bear!

Adapted from *Not THIS Bear!* by Bernice Myers

Little Herman was on his way to see his aunt.
It was very very cold. To keep warm, Herman
pulled himself down inside his long furry coat.
He pulled his big furry hat down over his eyes.
He looked just like a bear. And that is just what
a passing bear thought.

"You must be my Cousin Julius!"
said the bear. Grabbing Herman by the hand,
the bear ran with him to her cave.

"Look who I found in the woods!" the bear shouted.

All the bears ran over and hugged Herman.

"Cousin Julius, Cousin Julius!" they shouted.

"My name is Herman," said Herman.
But no one even heard. They were so happy.

"I'm not a bear . . . ," Herman said.
Again no one heard him. They were getting ready
to eat.

Everyone had soup. All the bears lapped it up.
Herman didn't. He used a spoon just as he had
learned to do. He happened to have it with him.
What a surprise for the bears!

"My, my!" Big Brown Bear looked at Herman.
"How smart you are to learn a trick like that!"

All the bears clapped.

Poor Herman. He wasn't a bear.
He was a little boy. He was sure of it.
The bears were just as sure that Herman
was their Cousin Julius.

"So," thought Herman, "I'll just show them
I'm really a boy!" He began to sing. He tied
his shoes. Then he stood on his head. He did
all the things boys and girls learn how to do.

The bears still thought Herman was a bear.

"What a smart cousin we have,"
said Big Brown Bear. "He knows so many tricks."

She yawned and went outside. Looking
at the sky, she said, "It's winter. Don't forget.
We sleep for at least two months."

"Two months!" said Herman. "I only sleep
one night at a time. In the day I go out and play.
I'm sure not sleeping through the winter months!"

"But all bears do," said a little bear.

"Not THIS bear," answered Herman.
"I like winter," he said. "I like to go sledding
and to skate. I like to drink warm milk.
I like to make big tracks in the snow.
Anyway, I go to school."

There was a long pause. No one said a word.
Then Big Brown Bear spoke. "Maybe you aren't
a bear after all. You know, you don't even have
a nose like a bear."

"Look!" shouted a bear, as he took off
Herman's furry hat and coat. "He's not a bear
at all."

"See, I am a boy," Herman said.

Papa Bear laughed. "That's the best trick of all. And the trick was on us."

Herman put on his furry hat and coat again. He said good-by to all the bears. He began to walk to his aunt's house. He was just about to leave the woods when a big black bear jumped out from behind a tree.

Running to Herman, the bear shouted, "Cousin Bernard, Cousin Bernard . . ."

Herman was smart. He ran just as fast as he could out of the woods.

What's It All About?

Poor Herman! He did not want to sleep through the winter. Did you know that bears sleep through the winter? You will read more about what bears do in the winter.

TAKE A FIRST LOOK

Look at the next page. What is the title of the story? Now look at the picture. What do you think this page is about?

FIND THE KEY IDEAS

Read the two smaller titles on the next page. These small titles are called headings. Each one tells about a part of the story. What is the first part of the story about? What is the second part of the story about?

READ CAREFULLY

Now read the story about bears in winter. What part tells about the bear getting fat? What is the heading of that part? What is the heading of the part about the bear waking up? What part tells about the bear being hungry? Which paragraph tells about the picture?

Hibernation

Getting Ready for Winter

This grizzly bear is getting ready to sleep for four months. He will sleep through the winter. This sleep is called *hibernation.*

To get ready for winter, the grizzly bear eats a lot. He gets fat. This fat helps keep him alive during hibernation. His furry coat helps him keep warm.

The Long Sleep

The grizzly bear does not always stay still when he hibernates. He moves around a little bit. Sometimes he looks for food. But he is fat. He does not need to look for much food.

When spring comes, the grizzly bear wakes up. He looks for food again. He is hungry after being asleep for so long!

ADVENTURES OF ISABEL

Isabel met an enormous bear,

Isabel, Isabel, didn't care.

The bear was hungry, the bear was ravenous,

The bear's big mouth was cruel and cavernous.

The bear said, Isabel, glad to meet you,

How do, Isabel, now I'll eat you!

Isabel, Isabel, didn't worry;

Isabel didn't scream or scurry.

She washed her hands and she straightened her hair up,

Then Isabel quietly ate the bear up.

Ogden Nash

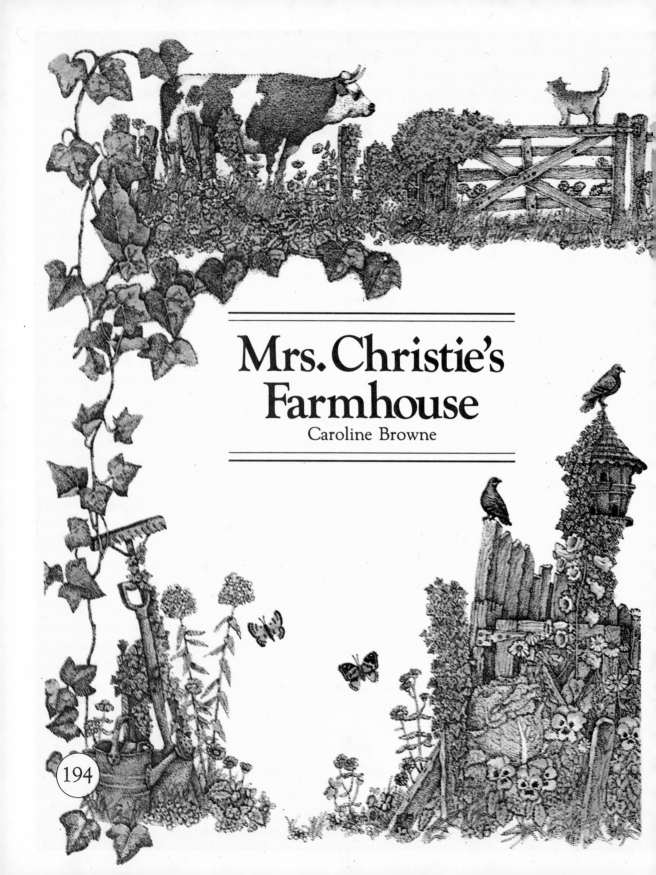

Mrs. Christie's Farmhouse

Caroline Browne

Mrs. Christie and Rachel wanted to live
in the country. Mrs. Christie knew of
a small farmhouse where they could live.
They packed up everything and took a train
to the country. They walked from the train station,
smelling the wild plants. They saw apples
growing on the trees. They were sure that
they would be happy in the country.

Soon they came to a gate. Behind the gate
was the farmhouse. A rooster was in the yard.
A cow stood far off on a hill. A goat was
in the wild garden, eating beets. Two hens
were near the back of the house. The farmhouse
looked nice and warm. Most of all, Mrs. Christie
and Rachel liked the wild garden.

195

Near the farmhouse stood the King's
castle. The King looked out the window.
He could see Rachel as she worked in the garden.
The King was a very organized man.
He did everything at just the same time
every day. His people stood in neat rows.
Every plant in his garden grew as tall
as the others. The castle was so organized
that the King had nothing to do. The King
was bored.

One day the King looked out
from the castle. He saw the farmhouse
and the garden. He saw all the animals
running around.

"That farm needs to be organized,"
he said. "It needs new trees, new cows,
and new fences all in a row."

At nine o'clock on the dot the next morning,
the King set off. He was on his way
to the farmhouse. With him went a long line
of gardeners.

Mrs. Christie met them at the gate.

"Good morning," said the King, for he was a kind man. "I am the King. You need to be organized, and I've come to do it."

"Thank you," said Rachel, "but we are happy just the way we are."

"Nonsense," said the King. "Everyone should be organized."

"Well, you can try," said Mrs. Christie, "but I don't think it will work."

The King looked on as the gardeners began to work.

"Those geese need to be put there," said the King. "The beets should be planted here. A new shed should be put just there."

As fast as the gardeners planted, the hens dug up the seeds. The goat ran after one of the gardeners. The rooster pecked at another. The cows crushed the beets.

At first the King was very cross. He looked at everyone running around. Then he began to laugh.

When the King had stopped laughing,
he called to Mrs. Christie.

"I never knew that not being organized
could be so much fun! Please may I come again?"

"Yes, you may," said Mrs. Christie.
"Rachel and I would like that."

"Good," said the King. "I will come
at three o'clock on the dot every Wednesday."

But he thought it might be fun
to be a little bit late sometimes.

Animals in Danger
Cara Lieb

Mrs. Christie had many animals
on her farm. She and Rachel took care of
the animals. They helped keep the animals
out of danger.

Not all animals live on farms. Most animals
live out in the wild. They don't have people
to take care of them when they are in danger.

Different animals get out of danger
in different ways. Some animals can scare
an enemy away. Bears make a loud sound.
They growl to scare an enemy away.

Many animals hide from danger.
A fawn is a baby deer. A fawn can hide well.
Look at this fawn. Can you tell why
a fawn sitting in the woods is hard
to see?

Some animals can trick an enemy.
An opossum can fool a fox. When an opossum
sees a fox, the opossum lies down. It stays
very still. The opossum looks dead. Then
the fox goes away. The opossum is safe.

Most animals do not fight an enemy.
They do not hide from an enemy.
They run away! Bullfrogs jump away.
When they are in danger, they jump.
See what happens to an old bullfrog
in the next story.

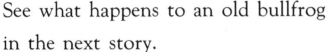

THE OLD BULL FROG

Berniece Freschet

It was a hot day. Bees hummed.
Big white clouds moved slowly across the blue sky.
A bird flew down. She sat on top of a plant
by a pond and sang a song.

The old bullfrog squatted on a rock. He was
lying in the sun. He was a giant of a water frog.
He had lived at the pond for many years.
The old bullfrog was very wise. That was why
he had lived so long.

A little while ago he had shed his skin.
Now his new green coat was sleek and smooth.
He liked the feel of the sun on his new skin.
The old bullfrog looked asleep. But he was not
really asleep.

He saw the red squirrel jump from tree to tree.
He saw the fat geese walk up to the pond. He saw
the little deer come down to drink.

But the old bullfrog did not see the heron.
The heron walked slowly along the side of the pond.
The heron was looking for something to eat.
Most of all, she liked to eat frogs. She moved
very slowly and with great care.

First the heron lifted up one long leg.
She stopped. Then, slowly, she put it down.
She lifted up her other long leg. Very slowly
she put it down. One had to be looking
right at her to know she moved at all.
When she stood still in the tall plants,
it was hard to see her.

Quickly, her long neck snapped down.
Her mouth opened, and she grabbed a fish.
But she was still hungry.

She stepped slowly along the side of the pond.
She moved toward the bullfrog.

205

Slowly the heron lifted one leg.

The squirrel stopped climbing.

The deer lifted her head from the water.

The heron put her leg down. Slowly
she lifted her other leg.

The owl in the big tree shut one eye.

A fly moved slowly across a leaf.

The heron took another step. She
was getting close now.

The bullfrog looked asleep.

Now the heron was very close.
She drew back her long neck.
Her mouth opened.

More quickly than an eye can blink,
she struck!

A bird cried out.

Plop! The old bullfrog jumped
into the water. He quickly swam away.

He had looked asleep. But
he had not really been asleep.

The old bullfrog was wise.
That was why he had lived so long,
here at the pond.

Vocabulary: Word Identification

Write each sentence, using the correct word.

1. The bears' _____ coats keep them warm.

smart   castle   furry

2. Where did you _____ to read so quickly?

lift   learn   wild

3. The _____ worked for months planting seeds.

gardener   sure   stepping

4. The squirrel moved very _____ up the tree.

wild   month   slowly

Vocabulary: Vocabulary Development (classification)

Write the word that does not belong with the others.

5. castle   sure   farmhouse   home

6. moved   walked   bored   stepped

7. month   day   year   gardeners

8. pushed   spoke   told   talked

Write the answer to the question.

Mrs. Christie's farmhouse is in the country. The farmhouse is small. The farmhouse is painted white. The King's castle is in the country. His castle is huge. The King's castle is made of white stone.

9. How are the castle and the farmhouse different?

They are in different places.

They are different sizes.

They are different colors.

Write each sentence, using the correct word.

Decoding:
Consonant sq(u),
Contractions
with have,
Plural
possessives

10. The geese _____ when they saw the fox.

learn   packed   squawked

11. _____ never seen a real heron.

We're   I've   I'm

12. The pigs' _____ squealed when the pigs fell.

yawn   mother   those

NOISES
IN THE WOODS
Judi Friedman

How to See Animals

Many animals live in the woods. Most of us
never see them. The animals are afraid of people.
They run away.

Some animals will not run away if you are very still.
Try not to talk. Listen for noises. Then try to find
the animal that is making the noises.

Move very slowly. Try not to walk on sticks
or dry leaves. Walk with care so you do not fall.
Move when you hear the animal's noise. Stop
when the noise stops. The animal may hide if he
hears you. He may think you will hurt him.

Some animals' eyes are on the sides of their heads.
They may not seem to be looking at you, but they can
still see you. Try to move when the animal's head is
turned away from you.

The animal may run away if he sees you.
Try not to move quickly.

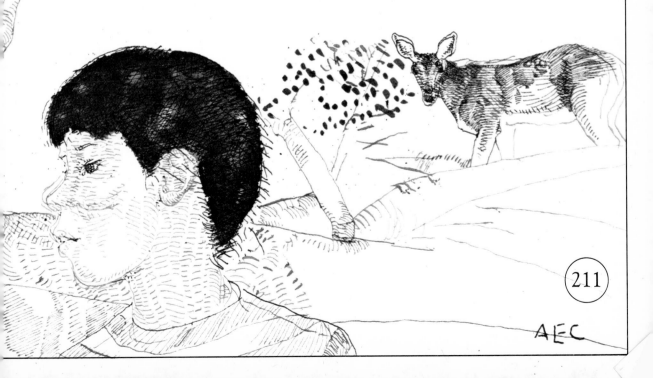

AEC

An animal might run away if he smells you.
Try to smell like things in the woods. Rub yourself
with something like pine needles. Don't be afraid.
When you are afraid, you give off a different smell.
Some animals will not like it. They might run away.

Animals will not hurt you when you just look
at them. Do not put your hands near wild animals.
If you do, they might think that you will hurt
them. They might bite you.

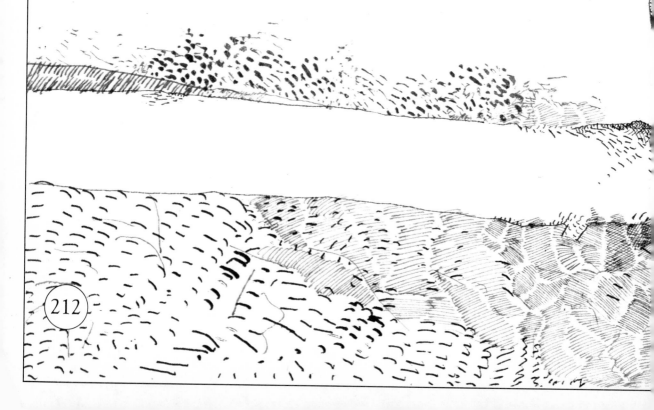

In the Daylight

Try going into the woods while the sun is up.
You might ask someone to go with you. Sit down and
listen.

You may hear something near the base of a tree.
Brown leaves may fly up. Walk slowly over to them.

The noises might sound as if they are being made
by a big animal. There is nothing to be afraid of.
A little head may pop out. It may be just a small bird.
She eats worms. She kicks up dry leaves to find them.

AEC

There are sounds in the sky, too. Look up!
You may see some crows. They may be flying around
and around.

You might want to find out why the crows
are making so much noise. Walk toward
the sounds. A big owl may be sitting in a tree
near the crows' nests. Owls eat baby crows.

Many animals live in or near water. Ponds and lakes are good places to see animals. Some frogs make big, deep noises in the summer.

Listen for the big noise of the bullfrog. Find out where it is coming from. Look for the bullfrog's yellow throat, which moves in and out when he makes noise.

The frog will splash if he jumps into the water. Look down into the water. He may be under some plants.

AEC

Guess Who?

Spring is a good time of year to listen for noises. Many animals are looking for mates. Other animals have a new baby to take care of. They are all looking for food after the long winter.

Try sitting outside on a spring night. Sit in the woods near a pond or a lake. You may hear these sounds.

"Splash! Splish, splash."

"Oh-o-o-o-o."

"CRACK!"

"Creeeeeeeeeeeak."

Guess what is making those noises!

AEC

Charts

One day May went for a walk in the woods. She wanted to remember what she saw. She made some pictures and a chart. The title of her chart is, "Animals I Saw in the Woods."

Look at May's chart on the next page. At the top of each column, she wrote a heading. May wrote the names of the animals she saw in one column. In the next column, she wrote how many of each animal she saw. In the last column, she wrote the times she saw the animals.

Suppose you wanted to know if May saw any fish. First, find the heading "Animal Name." Look down that column. Do you see the word *fish*? Now look across that row. The number 5 means that May saw five fish. The number 3:40 tells what time May saw the fish.

Use the chart to answer these questions. Did she see any bears? How many deer did May see? What time did May see the deer?

Animals I Saw in the Woods

Animal Name	How Many	What Time (P.M.)
Bullfrog	6	3:30
Fish	5	3:40
Owl	1	4:00
Squirrel	7	4:15
Heron	1	4:20
Deer	3	4:30

A Nest of Wood Ducks

Evelyn Shaw

It is spring in the woods. On a quiet lake
two fat birds swim side by side. They are wood ducks.

The male wood duck is called a *drake.*
He has bright feathers that shine in the sun.
The female wood duck is called a *hen.* Her feathers
do not shine. These wood ducks are mates.

The hen flies up to a tree. There is a
small hole in the side of the tree. The hen
squeezes through the hole.

Inside the hole it is dark and quiet.
The hen's nest is here. The nest is made of feathers
and bits of leaves. The hen has laid one egg each
day for eight days. She covers the eggs with
feathers and leaves. They can't be seen by animals
that might eat them.

Now the hen will stay in the nest.
For about a month she will sit on the eggs.
This will keep them warm. The leaves and feathers
will keep them warm, too. Inside the eggs,
baby ducks will begin to grow. The hen sits
on her eggs most of the day and all of the night.

Days pass by. A baby duck is growing
inside each egg. Its food is the egg yolk.
The yolk is the yellow part of the egg.

After a month the yolks are gone. The ducklings
are big enough to hatch. They begin to turn
inside the eggs.

One duckling begins to crack open its shell.
This is called *pipping.* Another duckling
pips its shell, and another, and another. In a while,
all the eggs have hatched. The ducklings' feathers
are wet and sticky.

The next day the ducklings are dry. Their feathers are soft and fluffy.

Plee. Plee. Plee. The ducklings call to each other and jump up and down. They are ready to leave the nest. They are ready to swim and to learn how to find food.

The hen looks out of the hole. She does not see any animals. When she is sure it is safe to go out, she flies down to the lake.

Kuk, kuk, kuk, kuk, kuk. She is calling the ducklings.

Inside the tree nest, the ducklings hear her.
They hop up and down. One duckling climbs up
to the top of the hole. The duckling looks out.
Then it spreads its wings and jumps down onto the
water. Splash! The duckling swims to its mother.

Then another duckling jumps down,
and another, and another. Splash, splash, splash!
All the ducklings swim to the hen. Then she swims
away with the eight ducklings close behind her.

225

Now the hen and ducklings will live on the lake. The drake flew away before the ducklings hatched. The hen will take care of the ducklings.

Many animals like to eat ducklings. The hen looks out for these animals. She listens for strange noises.

For about two months the ducklings stay close to their mother. They listen to her calls. They stay with her everywhere she goes.

The ducklings try to hide from animals that may eat them. On the lake they dive under the water. On land they sit close to the ground and do not move.

Days pass by. The ducklings are growing bigger. Their baby feathers fall off, and they grow flying feathers. Now they do not need the hen to take care of them. They can fly.

Soon they join other wood ducks and fly away for the winter. The hen goes, too.

The next spring a young hen flies to the lake.
A drake is with her. They are mates. The hen
is looking for a nest. She looks into holes in the trees.

The young hen goes into one of the holes.
Inside it is dark and quiet. There are feathers and
bits of leaves in the hole. It is an old nest.

The young hen picks this place to lay her eggs.
It is a special place. It is the nest where she hatched
last year.

THE GOOSE THAT LAID GOLD EGGS

Genie Iverson

Act One

STORYTELLER: The sun is going down.

Night is near. In an old farmhouse,

a man and a woman are sitting

by the fire. A young girl comes

into the room with wood.

A boy puts a pot on the fire.

WIFE: Is the work done for the day?

I feel a chill in the air.

GIRL: Well, we have wood for the night.

BOY: The chickens are in the shed. And

they've had their feed, and water, too.

HUSBAND: Yes, but what about the old gray goose?

Did she get her feed today? I don't

know what to make of her these days.

She sits near that back fence all day

long! Something must be happening.

WIFE: Is Grandpa still working in the garden?

It's time for him to come in.

GIRL: I'll call him.

229

Act Two

STORYTELLER: It is morning. The day is cool and
bright. The husband puts on
his hat and goes outside. He gets
a bag of feed from the shed.

HUSBAND: Where are you this morning,
my old gray goose?

GOOSE: I'm where I am every morning—
on my nest. (*The goose flies
from her nest to the husband.*)

HUSBAND: I've brought some feed for you.
What do you have for me?

GOOSE: You know what I always lay—one egg a
day. I lay one egg, one beautiful egg.
(*She begins to eat. The husband goes to the
nest. He stops in surprise.*)

HUSBAND: What have you been up to,
my old gray goose? What kind of egg
is THIS?

GOOSE: You know what I always lay—one egg
a day. I lay one egg, one beautiful egg.

HUSBAND: Yes, but this egg is special!
Look at the color! See how big it is!
Never have I found an egg
like this in your nest.

GOOSE: Yes, it is a special egg. (*She keeps on eating.*)

HUSBAND: (*He picks up the egg.*)
This egg is as yellow as gold.

GOOSE: Yes, I know it is. I laid it myself.

HUSBAND: But this egg IS gold—REAL GOLD!
(*The goose nods and keeps on eating.*)

HUSBAND: Everyone! Come see what the old
gray goose has done!

231

(The wife, boy and girl, and grandpa come running from the house.)

WIFE: What's all this about?

GIRL: What has happened, Papa?

BOY: Did the old gray goose hatch one of her eggs?

GRANDPA: Great balls of fire, what's going on?

(The husband holds up the egg.)

HUSBAND: Look. Take a close look. This egg is GOLD. The old gray goose has laid a gold egg!

GRANDPA: You're RIGHT. Sure as frogs are green, that egg is gold—REAL gold.

GIRL: What a wonderful egg!

WIFE: What a wonderful GOOSE!

BOY: Will she do it again tomorrow? Will she lay another gold egg?

HUSBAND: We'll find that out tomorrow. Now I'm off to the village. I'll trade this egg for things we need.

232

Act Three

STORYTELLER: Each day the goose laid one gold
egg. Each day the man walked to
the village. He went to trade the
gold egg for something he needed.
One day he came home with
a new cow. Another day he
came home with two pigs.
Each day they had something new
at the farm. Each day he came
home with all kinds of good food.

WIFE: The old gray goose is kind to us.
Now we have a cow, pigs, and goats.
We have good food to eat. We have more
than we need. And it's all because the
old gray goose lays one gold egg each day.

HUSBAND: Yes, the old gray goose is kind to us.
But I don't like to wait for the eggs day
after day. I don't like to go to the
village each day.

WIFE: How can you say such a thing?

BOY: Think of the milk from the cow, Papa.

GIRL: Think of the goats.

GRANDPA: How much do you want? Be patient.
Take care of that old gray goose, and
she'll take care of you.

HUSBAND: I don't like to wait for the eggs. I am
not a patient man. That goose must
be stuffed with gold eggs. If I kill her
now, think of what we would have!

WIFE: KILL the goose! How can you think
of hurting that goose?

HUSBAND: If I kill her, I can have the eggs
NOW! I can have them RIGHT NOW!
Then I won't have to wait any more.

WIFE: You must learn to be patient, husband!
Be happy with things as they are.

GRANDPA: That's right. You know what that
goose is always saying about its eggs.
"I lay one egg a day, one beautiful egg."

BOY: Don't, Papa! Please! Don't kill
the goose.

WIFE: Be patient!

HUSBAND: Don't tell ME to be patient.

GRANDPA: Be happy with what you have today, or
you may be sorry tomorrow.

HUSBAND: We'll see about that. (*He leaves the house.*)

235

Act Four

STORYTELLER: All is quiet at the farmhouse.
The mother, the boy, and the girl sit
together in the house. They are
waiting and waiting. Time passes
slowly. At last Grandpa comes
into the room.

GRANDPA: He did it. The goose is dead.

WIFE: He shouldn't have done it!
He shouldn't have done it!

(*The man walks slowly into the room.*)

WIFE: You killed the goose?

236

(*The man looks down at the floor. He nods his head.*)

WIFE: You killed the goose that laid one egg a day, one beautiful egg, one beautiful gold egg?

HUSBAND: (*He nods his head again.*) There was not one gold egg inside— not one. I am a fool. (*The wife nods her head.*) I had a wonderful goose, but I wanted everything at once. Now I have nothing. I was not patient. Grandpa was right. Be happy with what you have today. You may be sorry tomorrow.

Vocabulary:
Word
Identification

Write the words in the order that makes a sentence.

1. always   goose   Grandpa   feeds   the

2. pond   Ducks   splash   to   like   in   the

3. Children   move   quickly   can

4. nest   its   flies   The   to   hen

Vocabulary:
Vocabulary
Development
(classification)

Write the word that tells how the underlined words are alike.

5. <u>gold</u>   <u>yellow</u>   <u>orange</u>
   homes   colors   people

6. <u>duck</u>   <u>goose</u>   <u>owl</u>
   games   rooms   birds

7. <u>three</u>   <u>eight</u>   <u>seven</u>
   names   numbers   noises

8. <u>squirrel</u>   <u>badger</u>   <u>rabbit</u>
   animals   places   people

Think about "Noises in the Woods" and "A Nest of Wood Ducks." Write the answer to the question.

Comprehension: Comparison

9. How are the two stories alike?

Both stories tell about hatching eggs.

Both stories tell about animals and where they live.

Both stories tell you how to listen for animals.

Write the word that does not belong with the others.

Decoding: Consonants *scr, spr, str, sq(u), wh;* Inflection *-er*

10. screech   squeal   young   whine

11. taller   bigger   higher   better

12. spring   stripe   summer   winter

13. brook   pond   page   stream

Henry Possum

Harold Berson

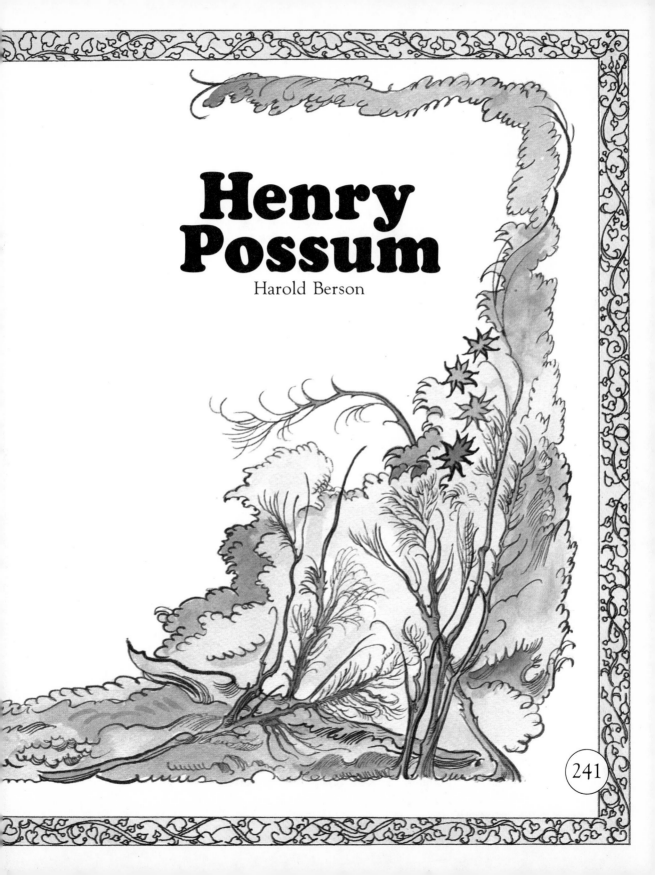

One day a mother possum took her five children off her back. She lined them up in front of her.

"It is time you learn to play dead," she said. She rolled over and lay very still on the ground.

"Now you try," she said. And one by one all of her children rolled over and played dead.

All, that is, except Henry. He was humming and watching butterflies.

"Henry," said his mother, "come here."

"And she gently laid him on the ground
and tried to make him lie still. But it was no use; Henry
kept on humming.

"You'll never fool anyone," she scolded.

"What will you do if a bear comes after you?

Or a fox?

Or a bobcat?"

"I never thought of that," said Henry.

"It could happen," she warned. She put all
five children onto her back. Slowly she carried them
up into the trees.

"Hold on tight," she said, "you especially, Henry."

As the possum family moved from
branch to branch, Henry felt warm against his
mother's fur. He gazed at the leaves against the sky.

He spied a ladybug crawling along a twig.

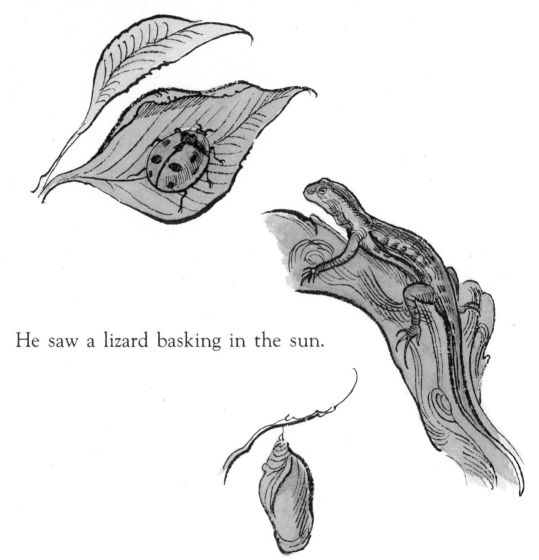

He saw a lizard basking in the sun.

He caught sight of a caterpillar spinning its cocoon.

He saw a woodpecker tapping for grubs and a
squirrel darting through the branches.

Then his twitching nose caught the scent of
honeysuckle below them. It was such a sweet
and lovely smell that he stretched down for more.
He stretched so far that he slid off his mother's
back and fell into the honeysuckle.

Henry just lay there, enjoying the smell. When
he realized he was all alone, he looked up into
the branches. His family was nowhere in sight.

251

Henry climbed out of the tangled
honeysuckle. He looked around. The woods
seemed very large. As he wandered among
the trees, he began to hum to keep
from being frightened. The more frightened
he felt, the louder he hummed.

253

"Well, I never," said a voice to Henry.
Henry looked up and saw a magpie
rocking on a branch.

"Have you seen my mother?" asked Henry.

"No," said the magpie, "I haven't. But
here—take this shiny new flute. It will
keep you company. My nest is such a mess
that I can hardly turn around."

"You're very kind," said Henry.

Henry wandered through the woods,
looking for his mother and tooting
on his shiny new flute, until he saw a beaver
building a dam.

"Have you seen my mother?" called Henry.

"No, I haven't," replied the beaver. "I have
been busy building my dam. But if you want to play
that flute, you'd better learn rhythm like this."

And his tail went slappity slap, slap,

slappity, slap, slap, against the mud.

"That's wonderful," said Henry.

He went on his way, repeating the rhythm on his flute. He heard a robin singing in a tree.

"Have you seen my mother?" asked Henry.

"No," sang the robin, "but if you're going to play that flute, you need to learn trills like these. Tra-lalalalala, tra-lalalalala, tra-lalalalala."

"Oh, how beautiful," said Henry.

Henry went deeper into the woods, playing trills on his shiny new flute. He saw a bullfrog sitting in a marsh.

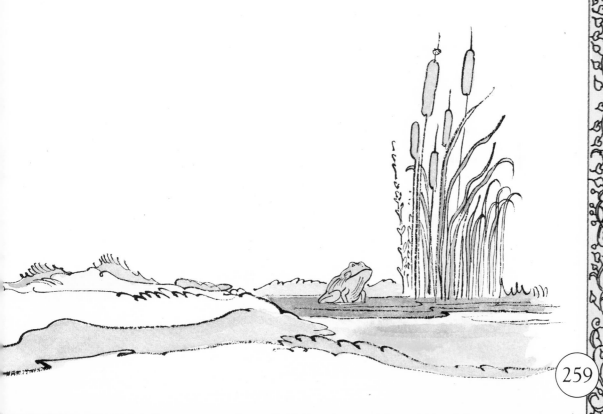

"Have you seen my mother?" asked Henry.

"No, I haven't," croaked the bullfrog. "But if you would like to play deep, round notes on that flute, just listen to me."

"Bro-ak, bro-ak, bro-ak," came the deep, round sound from the bullfrog's throat.

"That's different," said Henry.

He walked even deeper into the woods. He saw a wise old raccoon sitting in a gum tree.

"Have you seen my mother?" asked Henry.

"Yes, I have," said the raccoon, "she's
been looking all over for you. Why don't you
stay in one place and play your flute.
Your mother will surely come to see who
is making music."

Henry found a little hill nearby. He played
everything he had learned on his flute.

He played the beaver's slappity slap, slap,

the robin's tra-lalalalala,

and the bro-ak, bro-ak, bro-ak of the bullfrog.

He put them all together in a song of his very own. It was beautiful.

The robin and the raccoon, the beaver and
the bullfrog all knew that it was Henry playing his
flute. They came to listen. The magpie flew to a
nearby tree and proudly puffed her chest. One
by one all the creatures of the woods came
to see who was making music, even Henry's mother.

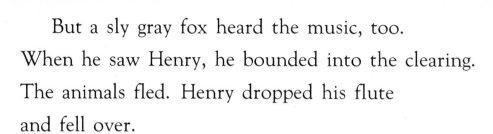

But a sly gray fox heard the music, too.
When he saw Henry, he bounded into the clearing.
The animals fled. Henry dropped his flute
and fell over.

The fox circled Henry. He sniffed at Henry.
But Henry lay perfectly still, and the
fox moved on.

"Henry!" shouted his mother as she got up off the ground. "You learned to play dead!"

"No, Ma," cried Henry. "I learned to play the flute. Listen."

He stood up, took a deep breath, and played as he had never played before. Hearing the music, the animals slowly returned to the clearing. As they listened to Henry's concert, each added its own voice to the melody.

GLOSSARY

Full pronunciation key* The pronunciation of each word is shown just after the word, in this way: **ab·bre·vi·ate** (ə brē′vē āt).

The letters and signs used are pronounced as in the words below.

The mark ′ is placed after a syllable with primary or heavy accent, as in the example above.

The mark ′ after a syllable shows a secondary or lighter accent, as in **ab·bre·vi·a·tion** (ə brē′vē ā′shən).

a	hat, cap	l	land, coal	u̇	full, put
ā	age, face	m	me, am	ü	rule, move
ä	father, far	n	no, in	v	very, save
b	bad, rob	ng	long, bring	w	will, woman
ch	child, much	o	hot, rock	y	young, yet
d	did, red	ō	open, go	z	zero, breeze
e	let, best	ô	order, all	zh	measure, seizure
ē	equal, be	oi	oil, voice	ə	represents:
ėr	term, learn	ou	house, out		a in about
f	fat, if	p	paper, cup		e in taken
g	go, bag	r	run, try		i in pencil
h	he, how	s	say, yes		o in lemon
i	it, pin	sh	she, rush		u in circus
ī	ice, five	t	tell, it		
j	jam, enjoy	th	thin, both		
k	kind, seek	ᵺH	then, smooth		
		u	cup, butter		

---

* Pronunciation key and Respellings are from *Scott, Foresman Beginning Dictionary* by E. L. Thorndike and Clarence L. Barnhart. Copyright © 1979 by Scott, Foresman & Co. Reprinted by permission.

A

al·ways (ôl′wiz or ôl′wāz) 1. all the time: They *always* clean their house on the weekend. 2. forever.

an·swer (an′sər) 1. to give a reply: She *answered* the teacher's question. 2. a reply.

an·y (en′ē) 1. a part. 2. some: I don't need *any* help. 3. every.

B

ban·jo (ban′jō) a musical instrument played by plucking or strumming its strings: The man played a lively tune on the *banjo.*

be·fore (bi fôr′) 1. in front of; ahead of: He cleaned his room *before* lunch. 2. in the past.

be·hind (bi hīnd′) in back of: The dog walked *behind* the children.

bet·ter (bet′ər) 1. healthier; no longer sick: You will feel *better* in the morning. 2. more than good.

Bre·men (brem′ən) a city in Germany: The city of *Bremen* lies between two rivers.

broth·er (bruTH′ər) a boy or man having the same parents as another person: My baby *brother* is two years old.

bull·frog (bul′frog′) a large frog that makes a loud croaking sound: On a quiet night, you can hear the *bullfrogs* at the pond.

bunch (bunch) 1. a group of things that are alike: She gave me a *bunch* of bananas. 2. things tied together. **bunches.**

C

cas·tle (kas′əl) a big house with high walls where royalty may live: The king built his *castle* on the top of a hill.

cen·ter (sen′tər) 1. middle. 2. a place where people get together for games and other activities: Does your family go to the *Center?*

change (chānj) 1. to become different: Some animals *change* color at different seasons. 2. to replace. **changed, changing.** 3. coins.

close (klōs) near; having little space between: Their house is *close* to ours. **closer, closest.** —**closely.**

coat (kōt) 1. outside clothing to wear over inside clothing: I put on my warm *coat* before going outside. 2. a thing that covers, for example, a *coat* of paint.

code (kōd) a secret way of writing: She wrote a note in a special *code.*

coin (koin) metal money, such as a penny or a dime: He dropped a *coin* on the sidewalk.

cold (kōld) 1. not warm; chilly: He became *cold* standing in the shade. **colder, coldest.** —**coldly.** 2. a sickness when your nose is stuffed up.

cos·tume (kos'tüm or kos'tyüm) a special outfit of clothes: I wore a ghost *costume* to the party.

cot·ton (kot'n) a soft, white, fluffy material that comes from a plant: We always keep *cotton* in our first-aid kit.

coun·try (kun'trē) 1. open land not in the city: My uncle lives on a farm in the *country.* 2. a nation. **countries.**

cov·er (kuv'ər) 1. to place over or around: You should have *covered* the food and put it away. 2. to hide. 3. something that covers.

D

dance (dans) 1. to move in time with music. **danced, dancing.** 2. a party where people dance: My friend and I are going to the *dance* together.

dan·ger (dān'jər) 1. a chance that harm may happen: There is *danger* in running too fast on wet roads. 2. something that may cause harm.

dark (därk) 1. having no light. **darker, darkest. —darkly.** 2. nighttime: Please come home by *dark*.

dic·tion·ar·y (dik′shə ner′ ē) a book that tells the meaning of words: Let's look up the word we don't know in the *dictionary*. **dictionaries.**

dif·fer·ent (dif′ər ənt) 1. not the same: The books may look the same, but they are *different*. **—differently.** 2. unusual.

dike (dīk) a dam used to hold back water: The people fixed the leaking *dike*.

do (dü) to finish or complete: I have *done* the work already. **did, done, doing.**

don·key (dong′kē) an animal that looks like a small horse: The girl rode the *donkey* home.

drum (drum) a round musical instrument covered with skin on the top: She wants to play a *drum* in the band.

E

eight (āt) the number that comes right after seven and just before nine; 8: Six and two are *eight*.

emp·ty (emp′tē) 1. not full; containing nothing: My piggy bank is *empty*. **emptier, emptiest.** 2. to pour out the contents of. **emptied, emptying.**

en·e·my (en′ə mē) something that will hurt something else: The fox is the *enemy* of the opossum. **enemies.**

eve·ry (ev′rē) 1. each one: I wake up before my family *every* morning. 2. all that is possible.

F

farm (färm) 1. land used to raise crops and animals: My aunt has chickens, goats, and cows on her *farm*. 2. to raise crops or animals to eat or to sell.

farm·house (färm′hous′) a house built on farmland for farmers to live in: The farmer carried fresh milk from the barn to the *farmhouse*.

feath·er (feᴛH'ər) a light, thin growth on a bird's skin: When a duckling hatches, its *feathers* are wet.

fire (fīr) 1. a burning with flames, light, and heat: The campers cooked their supper over an open *fire*. 2. to take away someone's job. **fired, firing.**

fly (flī) 1. to rise up into the sky; to soar: The crow *flies* from place to place to find food. **flies, flew, flying.** 2. a bug with wings. **flies.**

fore·head (fôr'id or fôr'hed') the front of the head above the eyebrow: Her *forehead* felt warm to me.

four (fôr) the number that comes right after three and just before five; 4: My sister turned **four** yesterday.

fur·ry (fėr'ē) having a soft coat of hair or fur: A bear is a *furry* animal.

G

gar·den·er (gärd'nər) a person who works in a garden: The *gardeners* pulled weeds all day.

gold (gōld) 1. a precious yellow metal: She has a watch made of *gold*. 2. the yellow color of this metal.

goose (güs) a water bird with a long neck: I watched the *goose* swimming in the pond. **geese.**

grand·pa (grand'pä *or* gram'pə) grandfather: My *grandpa* likes to play sports.

H

hat (hat) something you wear on your head: The *hat* covered his ears.

hatch (hach) to come out from an egg: Six ducklings *hatched* from the six eggs.

hear (hir) to take in sounds through the ears; to listen to: He *heard* the teacher calling his name. **heard, hearing.**

277

hur·ry (hėr′ē) to rush; to move fast: If we *hurry*, we won't be late. **hurries, hurried, hurrying.**

hurt (hėrt) 1. to cause harm or injury: The loud noise *hurt* my ears. 2. a cut or wound.

hus·band (huz′bənd) a man who is married to a woman: Her *husband* likes to cook.

I

i·de·a (ī dē′ə) a plan or a thought: It was her *idea* to play baseball.

in·side (in′sīd′) within; in; in the inner part: When the lights are out, it's dark *inside*.

its (its) belonging to it: The book has lost *its* cover.

K

knit (nit) to make by joining loops of yarn together: I like to *knit* winter caps. **knit, knitting.**

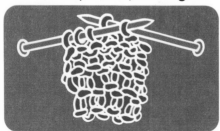

L

lad·der (lad′ər) a set of steps fastened to two long pieces of wood and used for climbing: Mom climbed up the *ladder* and saved the kittens.

laugh (laf) to make a happy sound when something is funny: They all *laughed* when they heard my joke.

learn (lėrn) to find out something new; to gain knowledge: The students *learned* how to read.

let's (lets) a short form of *let us*: *Let's* go to the zoo!

let·ter (let′ər) 1. a symbol from the alphabet: *Z* is the last *letter* in the alphabet. 2. a written message; a note.

lift (lift) to raise; to move higher: All together, we *lifted* the heavy box.

lose (lüz) 1. to not have something anymore; to not be able to find something: I have *lost* my new pen. 2. to fail to win. **lost, losing.**

M

mag·ic (maj'ik) a special power that makes things seem to appear or disappear: We saw a *magic* show at the party.

ma·gi·cian (mə jish'ən) a person who performs magic tricks: The *magician* pulled a rabbit out of a hat.

man·y (men'ē) a large number: There were *many* pets in the park. **more, most.**

match (mach) 1. to put things that are alike together: He *matched* his socks with his shirt. 2. a person or thing that is like another.

mel·on (mel'ən) a kind of fruit with a hard, thick skin: These *melons* are very juicy inside.

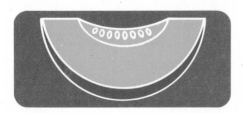

mid·dle (mid'l) 1. between the first and the last; at the same distance from all sides: The yellow lines are in the *middle* of the road. 2. a central area.

month (munth) a period of time; 28, 30, or 31 days: My birthday is in three *months.*

morn·ing (môr'ning) the first part of the day: I take a brisk walk every *morning.*

most (mōst) 1. the greatest amount. 2. to the greatest degree: She wanted to win *most* of all.

moth·er (muŦH'ər) 1. a parent who is a woman: My *mother* and my aunt look a lot alike. 2. a female animal that has babies.

move (müv) 1. to go from one place to another. 2. to cause to change place: The woman *moved* the bag from the table to the shelf. 3. to go to another place to live. **moved, moving.**

Mrs. (mis'iz) a title sometimes put in front of a married woman's name: *Mrs.* Jones is married to Mr. Jones.

Ms. (miz) a title put in front of a woman's name: *Ms.* Stone is our teacher.

mu·sic (myü′zik) sounds made by instruments or singing: I listen to *music* on the radio every night.

mu·si·cal (myü′zə kəl) having to do with music: That singer comes from a *musical* family. 2. a movie or play with music.

my·self (mī self′) my very own self: I can cook a meal by *myself.*

mys·ter·y (mis′tər ē) a happening that cannot be explained; a puzzle: Did you solve the *mystery* of your lost dog? **mysteries.**

N

name (nām) 1. to give a word by which someone or something is called: My brother was *named* for our grandfather. **named, naming.** 2. the word by which someone or something is known.

nev·er (nev′ər) not ever: He *never* rode a bus to school.

no·bod·y (nō′bod′ē) not one person; no one: When she answered the door, there was *nobody* there.

noise (noiz) a sound, often a loud one: She heard a loud *noise* outside her door. **—noisily. —noisy, noisier, noisiest.**

noth·ing (nuth′ ing) no thing; not anything: There was *nothing* on her desk.

num·ber (num′ bər) 1. amount. 2. numeral: I took a *number* and waited in line. 3. to assign a numeral to.

O

of·fice (ô′fis) a room in which to do work: Please come by my *office* tomorrow.

once (wuns) 1. at one time. 2. in the past. 3. as soon as: *Once* I saw her, I knew she was my friend. 4. one time and no more.

or (ôr) on the other hand; a word showing there is a choice: I will play either inside *or* outside tomorrow.

or·gan·ize (ôr′gə nīz) to make neat; to put things in order: Everything was *organized* for the party. **organized, organizing.**

our (our) belonging to us: We took *our* things and left.

out·side (out′sīd′) outdoors: May I go *outside* and play?

P

pair (per *or* par) a group or set of two things that belong together: He bought a new *pair* of shoes.

part·ner (pärt′nər) someone who shares work with someone else: My *partner* and I split up our work evenly.

par·ty (pär′tē) a group of people having a good time together: Would you like to come to my birthday *party*? **parties.**

pa·tient (pā′shənt) 1. to be able to wait calmly: I am always *patient* with him. 2. a person who goes to a doctor.

play·er (plā′ər) 1. someone who plays a game. 2. someone who plays a musical instrument: The trumpet *player* seems to play the loudest. 3.

an actor in a play.

po·ta·to (pə tā′ tō) a starchy vegetable that grows under the ground: We had chicken and *potatoes* for dinner. **potatoes.**

Q

quick (kwik) fast or swift: The students *quickly* cleaned up the room. **quicker, quickest. —quickly.**

qui·et (kwī′ət) not making any noise: The children became *quiet* when they heard a knock at the door. **quieter, quietest. —quietly.**

R

ra·di·o (rā′ dē ō) a machine that sends and receives sound: I listen to the news on the *radio*.

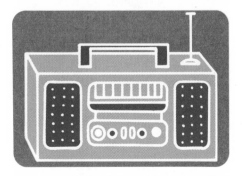

281

read·y (red′ē) 1. prepared: The punch is *ready* for the party. 2. willing. 3. at hand; available.

re·al·ly (rē′ə lē) 1. truly: Did she *really* go to play outside? 2. very.

right (rīt) 1. freedom to do a thing. 2. the opposite of left. 3. the honest thing to do. 4. without any wait: She did her homework *right* away. 5. not wrong; correct.

room (rüm *or* rûm) 1. a space with walls inside a building: My *room* is blue and white. 2. space.

roost·er (rü′stər) an adult male chicken: The crowing *rooster* wakes me up every morning.

round (round) having a shape like a ball or circle: A globe has a *round* shape. **rounder, roundest.**

S

say (sā) to speak; to put into words: He always *says* hello in the morning. **said, saying.**

school (skül) 1. a place where students go to learn: Reading is my favorite subject at *school.* 2. a large group of fish.

sci·ence (sī′əns) a study of finding facts by watching and doing tests: We are growing plants in *science* class.

sec·ond (sek′ənd) 1. coming after the first: He was the *second* one to finish his work. 2. a unit of time.

seem (sēm) to appear to be; to look like: The dog *seems* to understand its owner.

sev·en (sev′ən) the number that comes right after six and just before eight; 7: I saw *seven* people running down the street.

shape (shāp) 1. a form or figure: A ball has a round *shape.* 2. condition.

shoe (shü) a covering for your feet to wear over socks: Her *shoes* got wet in the rain.

sign (sīn) 1. a board with writing or pictures on it to give information: We couldn't read the road *signs* well at night. 2. a hint of something to come. 3. to write your name.

sis·ter (sis′tər) a girl or woman having the same parents as another person: The two *sisters* shared a room.

size (sīz) the smallness or largeness of something or someone: The crowd grew in *size* as time passed.

slow (slō) not fast; moving at a low rate of speed: The car *slowly* climbed the steep hill. **slower, slowest. —slowly.**

smart (smärt) 1. bright; able to learn quickly: My *smart* dog can do many tricks. **smarter, smartest.** 2. pain; hurt.

sor·ry (sor′ē) sad or unhappy: He is *sorry* to see the circus leave town. **sorrier, sorriest.**

spe·cial (spesh′əl) different; interesting; not ordinary: We will cook a *special* dinner. **—specially.**

splash (splash) to scatter or move water or another liquid: They could hear someone *splash* into the pond.

star (stär) 1. a bright point seen in the sky at night: It seems there are a million *stars* out tonight. 2. a famous person.

step (step) 1. to walk; to move the feet a short distance at a time: They *stepped* across the bridge. 2. to place the foot on. **stepped, stepping.** 3. a stair.

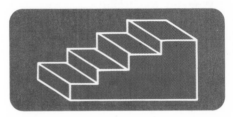

stom·ach (stum′ək) the part of the body that digests food: My *stomach* felt better after I ate lunch.

stop (stop) to quit moving: The car *stopped* at my house. 2. to bring an end to. 3. to block up. **stopped, stopping.** 4. an end. 5. a rest.

sto·ry (stôr′ē) 1. a real or make-believe telling of an event or happening; a tale: What *story* would you like to read? 2. one floor in a building. **stories.**

strange (strānj) odd, not ordinary: A zoo has many *strange* animals. **stranger, strangest. —strangely.**

straw (strô) 1. dried grain stems. 2. a small tube used to suck up drinks: I would like a *straw* with my milk, please.

stream (strēm) 1. a small body of moving water. 2. a flow of water, people, or things: They saw a *stream* of water coming from the dike. 3. to flow.

street (strēt) a road in a city or town: She lives on my *street.*

sure (shùr) certain; having a positive feeling: Are you *sure* that you finished your supper? **surer, surest.**

T

teach·er (tē′chər) a person who helps students to learn: My *teacher* is telling a story.

their (ℸHer *or* ℸHar) belonging to them: *Their* dog is looking for a bone.

think (thingk) 1. to have ideas; to use the mind: He was *thinking* about his homework. 2. to believe. **thought, thinking.**

throat (thrōt) the place inside the neck where a person swallows food: His sore *throat* feels better today.

tie (tī) 1. to lace together with a knot: She *tied* the leash to her puppy. 2. to make equal in a score. **tied, tying.** 3. a necktie.

tongue (tung) the part inside the mouth used for speaking, eating, and tasting: I bit my *tongue* by mistake.

U

un·der (un′dər) below; beneath: The ball rolled *under* the table.

up·stairs (up′sterz′ *or* up′starz′) 1. to the floor above; to the floor above the ground floor: He brought his toys *upstairs.* 2. in a place reached by stairs. 3. the upper floor.

use (yüz) 1. to put into action. 2. to consume, eat, or drink up. **used, using.** 3. —**used to** (yüst tü) did in the past: They *used to* live next door. 4. — (yüs) purpose.

W

wand (wond) a thin stick or rod: The magician used a magic *wand.*

wave (wāv) 1. to move back and forth: She *waved* a stick in the air. 2. to move your hand up and down in saying good-by. **waved, waving.** 3. moving water.

wear (wer or war) 1. to place on your body: He is *wearing* a new coat today. 2. to use up by rubbing away. **wore, worn, wearing.**

when (hwen) 1. at what time. 2. at the time that: I will give you the book *when* I am through with it.

wild (wīld) 1. living or growing in nature: They picked *wild* flowers in the field. 2. excited; not calm. **wilder, wildest.**

win·ter (win'tər) the season of the year right after fall and before spring: It is cold in the *winter.*

won·der·ful (wun'dər fəl) causing joy or happiness: They had a *wonderful* time on their trip. **—wonderfully.**

won't (wōnt) will not: He *won't* be going with you today.

word (wėrd) 1. a group of letters or sounds standing for an idea: He was so sad he didn't say a *word.* 2. a promise.

write (rīt) to make letters or words on paper or something else: Please *write* your name at the top of the page. **wrote, writing.**

Y

yarn (yärn) 1. threads twisted together to be used in knitting: I knit her some socks from this brown *yarn.* 2. a tale.

year (yir) a period of time. about 365 days: How many *years* have you lived there?

young (yung) not old; having lived a short time: The *young* colt looked for its mother.

(Acknowledgments continued from page 2)

Home." Appeared originally in the January 1980 issue of *Let's Find Out,* Part B, published by Scholastic Magazines, Inc. Used by permission of the author.

McClelland and Stewart Limited for the poem, and illustration, "Waiting at the Window" by A. A. Milne. From *Now We Are Six* by A. A. Milne reprinted by permission of The Canadian Publishers, McClelland and Stewart Limited, Toronto.

Eve Merriam for the poem "Catch a Little Rhyme" from *Catch a Little Rhyme* by Eve Merriam. Copyright © 1966 by Eve Merriam. Published by Atheneum. Reprinted by permission of the author.

William Morrow & Company, Inc., for the adaptations of "Helping" and "Farming" from *Partners* by Betty Baker. Text Copyright © 1978 by Betty Baker. By permission of Greenwillow Books (A Division of William Morrow & Company). Also for "Rock Stew" and "Serendipity," with illustrations, in *Mr. Brimble's Hobby and Other Stories* by Eve Rice. Copyright © 1975 by Eve Rice. Adapted by permission of Greenwillow Books (A Division of William Morrow & Company), and also by permission of the publisher in the United Kingdom, World's Work Ltd.

Scholastic Magazines, Inc., for "Not THIS Bear!" with selected illustrations, adapted from *Not THIS Bear!* by Bernice Myers, copyright © 1967 by Bernice Myers. Used by permission of Scholastic Book Services, a Division of Scholastic Magazines, Inc.

Scott, Foresman and Company for the respellings on page 169. From *Scott, Foresman Beginning Dictionary* by E. L. Thorndike and Clarence L. Barnhart. Copyright © 1979 by Scott, Foresman & Co. Reprinted by permission.

Illustrators and Photographers: Linda Post, Kristen Dietrich, Post & Co., 1-9, 34-37, 64-69, 92-95, 118-123, 152-155, 168-169, 180-183, 190-191, 208-209, 218-219, 238-239, 273-286; Susan Spellman Mohn, 10-17; Eve Rice, 18-27; Jenny Rutherford, 28-33, 110-117; Carolyn McHenry, 38-41; Ann Grifalconi, 42-43; Laura Joffe Numeroff, 44-49; Gary Fujiwara, 50-55; International Stock Photo/Thode, 50; Woodfin Camp/George Hall, 51; Shostal Associates/Robert Abrams, 52; Shostal Associates/Alvis Upitis, 53 left; Shostal Associates, 53 right; Shostal Associates/Marie Mattson, 54 left; Bruce Coleman/Lee Foster, 54 right; Bruce Coleman/David Madison, 55 upper left; Black Star/B. & C. Alexander, 55 upper right; Shostal Associates/Julius Fanta, 55 center; Bohdan Hrynewych, 55 lower left; Peter Arnold/Bill O'Connor, 55 lower right; Cathy Bennett, 56-63; Kristen Dietrich, 70-75; Bernard Wiseman, 76-83; David Cain, 84-91; Richard Berry, 96-101; Dan Collins, 102-103; Stephen Ogilvy, 104-109, 156-161; Line illustration by E. H. Shepard copyright under the Berne Convention, 124-125; Lady McCrady, 126-131; Judy Pelikan, 132-143; Jack Kent, 144-151; Kiki, 162-167; Frank Asch, 170-179; Bernice Myers, 184-189; Maria Harvath, 192-193; 200-201; Caroline Brown, 194-199; Patrick Blackwell, 202-207; Alan E.Cober, 210-217; Tommy Soloski, 220-227; Michael Hague, 228-237; Harold Berson, 240-272;

Design, Ginn Reading Program
Creative Director: Peter Bradford
Art Director: Gary Fujiwara
Design Coordinator: Anne Todd
Design: Lorraine Johnson, Linda Post, Kevin Young, Cathy Bennett, Kristen Dietrich

CDEFGHIJ089876
Printed in the United States of America